Fish Head Soup and Sassafras Tea

by:
Ora Wills

Fish Head Soup and Sassafras Tea
Copyright ©2018 by Ora Wills. All rights reserved.

Published by:
Proper Publishing LLC.
www.properpublishing.info
theproperpublisher@yahoo.com
Cover and interior design
©2018 by Proper Publishing LLC.
If you're going to publish, do it properly.

Dedication

To my daughter,
Angela Kyle.

Contents

Today I'll take Mama's clothes to the laundromat for the last time to chase away the lingering reminders of her infirmities. She was proud on to the end, always denying the inadequacies of defunct body parts. She'd allow as to how Old Lady X smelled pissy and "Uncle Silas musta pissed in my bed" when Doris brought him down from New York last year, for how else could she explain the ammonia-laced effluvian that stung the eyes that hung about the room, seeping into the cracks and creeping into unknown crevices despite the daily application of chlorine bleach and sundry deodorizers.

I had been with Mama too long, observing her gradual decline, the slow erosion of her powers, the stripping away of all her defenses, leaving her naked in an alien land. The familiar had grown hostile and threatening as she embarked, fearful and hesitant on the last leg of her journey.

I was her companion, an unlikely choice, but the only one since circumstance had placed me here and her need kept me chained. I railed against such a fate, feeling abandonment and isolation as we toe danced a mad dance that must end with a gaping flower-decked hole.

For years Mama had seemed immortal---indestructible. She always was and always would be. In my early adolescence I had been terrified that somehow she would slip away some night, leaving me utterly alone, bereft of a female parent-

--abandoned---but she never did, and I grew to understand her hypochondria---her dizzy spells, her "hurtings around the heart," her headaches and "pains in the back of the head." Mama craved attention and if her aches and pains didn't elicit a response, she would pick a fight with whoever was present when her longing came.

"Mama" was actually my grandmother, inheriting the role of mother to me after my mother was killed in an auto crash on Christmas day, 1936. I was one year old. Mama took over the role of full-time mother after my aunt went to New York to marry a man she had met while there visiting a friend.

My earliest notions of Mother grew out of my relationship with Doris. When a window opens and I can see the past with perfect clarity, my earliest memories include Doris. I remember:

I sat in a small wagon. Dot-tee pulled the wagon and we went out into the woods up from the house to gather small twigs and branches to build a fire around the pot. It must have been autumn or winter. I was all bundled up and I can still hear the leaves crackle as Dot-tee walked and pulled me in the wagon. Dot-tee gathered the firewood and heaped it into the wagon in front of me and we headed back

****

Dot-tee took me to pick violets. They grew profusely in the woods behind the house. Under the

*pine tree and near the small oak tree, I ran,
gleefully snatching up the tiny purple flowers. One
day, as we headed back, Dot-tee said, "Baby, I can't
see." I was frightened, but I said "Don't worry, Dot-
tee, I will take you home." It was not until we
reached the outer edges of the plum orchard that
Dot-tee said, "I was only pretending, baby; I just
wanted to see if you could find the way home."*

****

*I lay curled under the light covers as flashes
of lightning illuminated the semi-darkness. Thunder
rolled and rain pelted the roof. I was vaguely aware
of the promise of approaching spring. The storm
would pass and a bright day dawn. The rattle and
clatter of dishes penetrated my consciousness. Papa
prepared to walk the three miles for another day of
work at the factory and Mama prepared breakfast.
Coffee and frying bacon smells wafted from the
kitchen. I was secure. I could sleep another hour.
The morning ritual I had awakened to since I could
remember continued. I drifted away. Dot-tee was
asleep in the other bed. I was safe.*

*Awakening, pushing back the fading
curtains, I gazed out on the familiar transformed.
The world glistened and shimmered. The wild
growth that enveloped our gray weather-beaten
house sparkled with light caught in raindrops
trembling on branches, dazzling the beholder. All
was fresh. All was new. Dot-tee was near.*

****

It was Doris who first took me out of the narrow circumference of my immediate world. We took a train to Union Springs, Alabama, stopping at Flomaton, a junction that sent cars filled with people to the faraway lands of New York, Chicago and Los Angeles. Blasts of steam whistles and puffs of smoke, fed the excitement in my blood, and though Union Springs, Alabama was barely a stone's throw from home, traveling there was as great an adventure as embarking on a voyage to China or England or France.

We changed trains at Flomaton and I watched in fascination as a short, black man with a gigantic knot on the back of his head uncoupled cars. The "all aboard" call sent Doris and me scurrying to our locomotive. We sat in a car with plush blue seats. Other trains moving past gave the distinct impression that we were in motion. Finally, the illusion of motion turned into reality and with a series of blasts, our train pulled out into the night.

In the morning we pulled into the station at Union Springs. Disembarking, I can vaguely recall several very Southern types moving along with us or sauntering along, heading toward us, going in the opposite direction.

In Union Springs I met my grandfather's people: His mother, Annie, a fossilized very black woman whose union with a white man had produced my grandfather and another son, while

her coupling with a white had produced his sister
Julie, a light-skinned woman with long, straight
hair. Julia's daughters, Lillie and Jean were the
products of her own liaison with another white.
Lillie and Jean were blue-eyed blonde types,
Lillie's hair being naturally curly and falling in
ringlets around her face. Jean's hair flowed in
natural ripples and waves.

I remember little of that first and only visit.
Only two incidents break through from that
remote time. Doris and Lillie, around the same
age, planned to go to a dance in Tuskegee. Fearful
of spending the better part of a night alone with
these strangers, I wailed and cried myself to sleep.
I felt I was being abandoned and left to fend for
myself, a stranger in a strange land.

Later in the week, Doris and Lillie had taken
bunches of crisp collard greens from the garden.
These they had picked and washed and put on the
stove to cook with ham-hocks or salt pork. As I
amused myself in another room, I heard snatches
of their conversation. One of them had looked in
the pot and gasped, discovering a fat, green
caterpillar. I heard them debating what to do.
They removed the worm and continued to boil the
greens for dinner.

At dinner that evening I dawdled over my
helping. The memory of the caterpillar took away
any desire to eat, collard greens not being one of
my favorite foods even without fat green
caterpillars and only God knows what else. As the
others savored the vegetables, I squirmed in my

9

seat and finally reaching into my plate with my hands, I squeezed the greens and cornbread, letting them ooze between my fingers.

Doris looked at me horrified. She scolded me harshly, finally snatching me up and giving me a few smacks on the behind. I howled at the injustice of my punishment. In later years, Doris told me that I had imagined the whole incident.

I no longer remember how long we stayed with Grandma Annie and Aunt Julia, but when I returned home, my small white biddy had turned into a fine full-feathered pullet with a bright red comb. When we drove up, it was standing near the treacherous Spanish bayonet that grew at the corner of Grandma's room.

When Doris was not in attendance, I was on my own.

****

Every day I constructed a make-believe world in the front yard. Others might see only a jumble of odd and horribly rusted, broken and misshapen junk, but to my five-year-old mind this crude disarray was the inside of a fine and elaborate house. In it lived an imaginary family and I was its mistress.

The boundary of this exquisite place was defined by four giant trees which served as corners---three pecan trees and one chinaberry tree, growing in such a way that if an imaginary line were drawn from each to the other, they comprised a giant square.

Anyone with a degree of perception about such matters could see the interior walls that separated each room from the other. In the space surrounding the chinaberry tree---the southeast corner of the house---the kitchen lay. The stove, the upper part of a real wood stove somehow standing against a tree, was where I prepared the scrumptious meals that I served to family and guests. In the warmer rested the evening's main course---a marvelously roasted fowl (in reality a dead bat that had somehow died there the night before).

The bedroom was the area extending from the first pecan tree in the southwest corner of the house. Here, depending upon whimsy, the children were put to bed with a lullaby or my own hair was put up for the night while I awaited the shadowy dream-figure who was my husband. The room was furnished with the doll bed that I had brought from our real house, a structure, what with its gray, decaying and powdery walls, in no way compared to the splendor of my imaginary abode.

The parlor extended from the northwest corner to the northeast and was furnished with whatever happened to be available, depending upon what Papa had been able to scrounge from various trash heaps he passed as he walked to work. Today, there was an enamel cover of something huge that was turned underside up.

Other unidentifiable refuse became whatever in my imagination I needed to concoct a fantasy.

The swept-clean dirt floor of the house was kept so by continuous sweeping with a broom, made either from branches of a nondescript kind of bush tied together with string or branches of dog fennel likewise tied together.

The floor was dappled by sunlight filtering through the wide leaves of the pecan tree or the lacy, profuse leaves of the chinaberry tree. An occasional breeze let in the bright blue of the sky.

Hours slipped away and the summer passed. Late in the summer the floor would be covered with crawly, fuzzy hairy worms fallen from webbed nests they made in the branches of the pecan tree. In the evenings Papa would tie rags to a long stick, saturate the rags with pungent kerosene, touch a match to the rags, poke the flaming rag-covered stick into the webs in the tree and web worms would rain to the ground, rolling away with undulating motion as I squealed and smashed them with my bare feet, the cold gray-green juice oozing between my toes.

****

It had been an unusual day. Usually we had few visitors during the week, unless you counted the vegetable man who from time to time appeared in his incredibly battered truck laden with bright red tomatoes, yellow squash, green corn with silken tassels, and sweet, ripe peaches.

Or the ice cream man whose tinkling bell signaled his passing and occasionally meant a tangy dreamsicle or an icy sharp popsicle.

That day, no sooner than the beds were made in Grandma's room, which contained two rocking chairs with plush maroon seats and served as what we called the living room, than two Jehovah's Witnesses came, spending an interminable time explaining and discussing scriptures with Grandma. Grandma finally gave them the nickel for the <u>Watchtower</u>, which she could not read, and they were on their way.

As soon as the Witnesses had cleared out, a traveling salesman drove up, carrying some kind of grip which he opened before too long, spilling out a vast array of brightly colored wares. These he spread on Grandma's chenille covered bed and proceeded to display. Mama and Doris were dragged reluctantly from the back, and we examined the goods before us. He kept returning to his jalopy, bringing an ever-mounting pile of goods into the room. Having no intention of buying any of the finery, the three grown-ups listened somewhat impatiently, but good-naturedly to the huckster's pitch. Excited by the bright colors and dreaming of owning some of the merchandise, I danced about in excitement. It was nearing four o'clock when the salesman, despairing of any hopes of a sale, gathered together his wares, and after several trips back and forth to his dusty mud-splattered car, drove away.

At some point during the salesman's pitch, Mama had managed to escape to walk to Coleman's store on Davis Highway to get something to cook for supper, leaving Grandma and me with the salesman. Doris had disappeared into the kitchen.

When the salesman left, I was still in a state of euphoria from the bright colors and the running stream of sales talk. I ran from Grandma's room, out the front door, and took a running, flying leap, grasping a slender wire that extended between two of the porch posts. Mama or Doris had hung clothes on the wire to dry. As I ran for the wire, both Grandma and Papa, who happened to be passing by the front porch, cried out simultaneously, "Don't swing on that wire, baby."

Their cries came too late. I had flung myself out, grasping the wire in both hands with my arms extended above my head. The wire tore loose from the posts, and I hit the ground with a thud, my right arm twisted beneath me, partially covered with semi-wet clothes, now ruined by clinging sand and trash from the yard.

Papa picked me up, and my right lower arm was twisted at an angle. Too stunned to cry, I tried to get back the breath the fall had knocked out of me. Doris had heard the commotion and come from the back and Mama, returning from Coleman's had come up shortly after. They all stood around me, Doris examining my arm. I tried to move the arm, but it refused to obey any signals.

14

"It's broke," Papa said. "We got to get this child to a doctor."

Doris and Mama gathered up their purses and put some shoes on me, and we started out up the road walking, Doris complaining that she hadn't had time to change to clean clothes. Afraid to undress me, they took me, wearing the faded cotton I had worn all day.

We waited for the bus on Davis Highway. We had no car. An eternity seemed to pass before the bus slowed to pick us up. I can't remember the bus ride too clearly, but we exited at Chase and Palafox Streets, downtown and walked two or three blocks to the Medical Center.

Mama and I waited in the Colored Waiting Room---a space the size of a closet, with straight-back chairs on either side. Dark, mournful looking Negroes sat motionlessly in each chair. Doris had gone somewhere, but after a long time, reappeared, and we all waited. We waited a long time and a couple of Negroes complained that the whites sitting in the spacious waiting room outside were always called first.

Eventually a nurse came and escorted us to a room. A doctor appeared and greeted me with a light banter I cannot recall. My dress was split; I was placed on a table, I suppose, and something was placed over my nose.

Somebody said, "Don't let her vomit on me," and I slipped out of consciousness and into a vivid dream.

I was picking brightly colored flowers on the slopes of a hill that ran down to Carpenter's Creek. I stood under a large oak tree at the foot of the hill and red, blue, and yellow flowers were sprinkled profusely on the hillside. I worked my way up the hill, stooping to snatch up the blossoms as I ascended. In one hand I held a bouquet of vivid blooms. The hillside was flooded with incredibly bright sunlight.

When I awoke, I was home. It was morning, and I was lying in Grandma's bed in the front room. A hard white cast covered my right arm, extending from above the elbow to my wrist.

Lost in Wonderland

I entered first grade late because of my broken arm. Mama, Grandma, and Doris kept me at home, thinking somehow that the cast on my arm had afflicted my brain. Actually, they thought that since my right arm was in a cast, I could not be expected to write the assigned lessons. I wore the cast for over a month, and when the doctors finally removed it, my arm was weak and stiff, and refused to straighten out. The doctors told me to carry buckets of sand, the weight gradually to stretch the cramped muscles and straighten my arm out.

By the time my arm stretched out, it was almost two months into the school year. Finally, Doris took me to the school, and always shy and silent with strangers, I was frightened and uncomfortable with the idea of spending most of the day halfway across the county with strange, dark children.

I had grown up alone, without the companionship of other children and had learned to entertain myself with whatever devices I could find. The only companions I had ever had other than chickens and rabbits and other wild things in the woods were a couple of children of friends of Doris---Tommy and Joyce---who infrequently were brought out to our house to play with me. Never having had to play with other children, I found these experiences decidedly unpleasant. A few white children lived nearby and occasionally I played with them.

Once Doris had carried me to an Easter Egg hunt sponsored by a social group. While the other children had scrambled about in a wild frenzy looking for the prize golden egg, I had stood bewildered in one spot and found not a single egg, and certainly not the golden one. Usually on Saturday before Easter, Doris dyed a dozen eggs and on Easter Sunday she hid them around the yard, and I found all of the eggs myself, having no one to compete with.

Doris wondered how I would fare in competition for grades and popularity in the school, being so skittish of other children.

When we finally reached Spencer Bibbs school, having taken a city bus to Davis and Jordan Streets, we walked about two blocks south and entered the school. Doris and I were taken to the first grade room and introduced to Mrs. Pike. She seemed nice, but I was uncomfortable having entered the room already filled with other children. They eyed me curiously. I stared at my shoes.

Finally, Mrs. Pike said, "See that work on the board, Orastine; can you read it for me?"

I looked at the board and read the words without stumbling. Doris had long ago taught me to read. Mrs. Pike said, "I don't think she'll have any trouble. She's a smart one."

I did not have any trouble with the lessons, but I never quite became accustomed to the other children. I learned four or five of them by name, but mostly I stayed to myself and was glad when Doris showed up at the end of the day to take me home. No children visited me as I lived too far away from their homes, and they really never got to know me.

I was embarrassed by Doris's bringing me to school in the mornings and coming for me in the afternoons as the other children seemed to come and go without anyone's assistance. I was sure the other children thought I was peculiar or a baby who could not be trusted to get around alone.

Later, after Doris married and left, I was even more mortified when Grandma took me to the school. She would find a house in the neighborhood and sit there all day waiting for school to be out and it was time to come for me. Grandma wore long dresses that swept the ground, had huge size 11 feet that she encased in long, "old lady" shoes, and I was constantly embarrassed when someone asked, "Is that old lady with the long dress on your grandma?"

Since there was no way to lie about our relationship, I admitted that she was. I wondered how I could tell the children how wonderful Grandma really was, and how generous, but I never did.

I made good grades in first grade but remember very little of the day to day events. In second grade I experienced my first real disappointment. Mrs. Francis was our teacher, and as Christmas neared, there was great excitement over the Christmas play.

The play had something to do with a little girl who received a box full of dolls. Since I was so shy, needless to say, I was not considered for the lead. I did so wish to be one of the dolls who would leap out of the giant box when it was opened.

One by one the doll characters were chosen. They would be the ones dressed in frilly dresses, wearing bright ribbons. I wanted one of the parts since the dolls were not required to speak, only to leap out and be beautiful. All of the doll girls were chosen, and I was not one. What I did in the play, I can't remember, I think I was among a group of nondescript children who sang a few carols.

The night of the play, I stared enviously as the lipsticked and rouged light-skinned "dolls" burst from the box. I never mentioned my disappointment to Mama, Doris or Grandma. I withdrew into my dreams as I stared into the fire or rocked on the front porch. In my dreams I was more beautiful than those painted dolls, my hair loosened from its tight braids, straightened and flowing. I was the fairy princess. If only they knew.

Elementary school was full of small disappointments. I had grown to know most of my classmates. They knew me and admired and envied my high grades, yet I did not belong.

Sometime around the end of second or third grade, Doris left for New York.

I remember there was much discussion back and forth with Mama and Papa over Doris's leaving. Papa said, "Why you want to go way up there to marry a man? You got men friends here. Why you want to go way up there?"

It was true that Doris had always had beaus. She was a lovely light-skinned young woman with long black hair and deeply dimpled cheeks. She had been her high school queen and had actually been married before.

Her husband had died tragically a brief time after the marriage, leaving her depressed and restless. After my mother was killed and after Doris's recovery from the same accident, she had resumed a social life and looked after me. Once when she had gone to a dance, I had wailed to be taken along, fearful of losing her.

The day before Doris left, I withdrew into a dream world and watched silently as preparations were made. The day Doris left I felt an increasing emptiness, and when she finally closed her suitcase and sat on it to snap the clasps shut, I choked back tears. Then the cab came and she kissed me, her perfume hanging in the air long after she had gone. I had been abandoned.

For two or three days. I held back the tears that trembled always close to the surface. Always a picky eater, I ate less than usual. On the third day, just before nightfall, as I walked behind the house, just outside the kitchen, I fell to the ground and hot tears surged up. I sobbed there on the hard ground for the longest time. Finally, the tears subsided and I went back into the house. I never admitted to Mama or Grandma that I missed Dottee, but for years I felt lost and alone, and eagerly awaited her answers to my letters and the Christmas box with something bought in that magical enchanted place—New York.

In fourth grade two disappointments left me more unsure of myself socially and caused me to withdraw further into the dreams with which I made life exciting and varied.

I convinced Mama to let me have a birthday party. Never having been to one nor given one before, I was a little fuzzy about how to proceed. Another girl in my class had passed out invitations to her birthday party at school, so I knew that one of the first steps would be to give out invitations.

For weeks after the idea dawned, my head was filled with elaborate plans, always a bit hazy, but always ending with the grandest of parties. I worried that our house was such a shabby one, but the desire for the party outweighed my misgivings about the sad condition of our house. We could always play outside in the yard where the best fun was to be had.

The week before the party, I wrote out the invitations and gave them to my classmates. The party was to be on Saturday, November 17, my birthday.

Saturday morning came, and it was a bone-chilling gray overcast day. The party was to begin at 3:00. For most of the day I was filled with both anticipation and dread. I helped Mama arrange the house as best I could. Around 2:00 I put on my nicest dress and waited. At 3:00 no one had arrived. I grew more and more anxious. Around 3:30 Dannie Aster Crumb's mother brought her in their car. Time passed slowly. Danny Aster and I played inside, the weather being too cold to go outside. By 4:00 no one else had shown up. Dark gray clouds hung over the entire county. Finally, Danny Aster and I ate the cake and drank whatever Mama had fixed. Although it had been fun playing with Dannie Aster, I was saddened that only one person had come.

Monday morning at school, Mrs. McCurdy asked how many children had come to my party. Only Dannie Aster raised her hand. Mrs. McCurdy made all of the other children apologize to me. I was even more mortified by their timidly walking to my desk and the perfunctory apologies. I vowed never to give another party.

In spring as we prepared for May Day, my second disappointment loomed.

Excitement ran high as we were picked for dances and the plaiting of the Maypole. Secretly, I longed to plait the pole, but was terrified that if I were chosen, I could not execute the intricate skipping in and out dance.

At last our class found out we would do a dance about rain and rainbows, called "Singing in the Rain," after the movie. The prettier and livelier girls were chosen to be the rainbow and would be dressed in bright pastel crepe paper dresses with ruffles and flowers. I was among a group chosen to be the rain. We were to dress in dull gray crepe paper streamers that supposedly, when we danced our little steps, looked like rain falling. I hated that costume. Somehow I got through the ordeal of the dance without a major blunder, though I knew my steps were clumsy. In my dreams, though, I was an exquisite ballet dancer, not a part of the rainbow, but the rainbow princess, out-dancing all of the others.

After my group performed, I wandered around the grounds from concession to concession, a little lost, but pretending to have fun.

Suddenly, I felt the urge to go to the bathroom. We were not allowed back in the building, and I didn't know what to do. On and on the festivities went. Finally, unable to contain the urge, I felt the water streaming down my legs and into my shoes. I kept wandering about, trying to look normal. No one ever noticed, and I never told Mama. As I was to do most of my life, I held in the disappointment, pain and embarrassment, a seven-year-old grade school stoic.

I continued to lose myself in day dreams. There were serial dreams that involved, myself woven into original adventures as comic book heroines or characters from radio shows. In one fantasy I was Wonder Woman. In another, a blond-haired girl detective and in still another, an Elizabeth Taylor-like creature, and finally an intrepid newspaper reporter who continually broke the "big story."

Exploring

In fifth grade, as spring brought the trees and flowering shrubs to life, Mrs. Presha, our teacher, thought that the city children would enjoy a "trip to the country." She asked Grandma if she could bring the whole fifth grade to our house. Where we lived was not rural in the sense of farming country, but there were certainly open spaces and woods aplenty. I was not comfortable with the thought of our dilapidated house, but the plans began to mushroom, and I could think of no way to stop them. We planned a day-long excursion. We would set out from the school in the morning and hike the distance from the school to our house. We planned comfortable clothes to wear, snacks to take along, songs to sing on the way to and from our destination. (I would not hike back, being already at home).

Everybody prepared what Mrs. Presha called a "walking salad"—diced apples, raisins, and nuts. We learned some songs to pass the time, and sometime in May, the whole fifth grade set out walking to our house.

The journey was simpler by foot than by the circuitous route I took by bus. We only had to walk straight out Davis, due north, about three miles, and turn onto our lane.

The day was sunny and warm. The long string of fifth graders set out (two combined classes). We plodded along, singing our little songs and munching on our walking salad, first past Jordan Street, then Maxwell, Bobe, Scott, Cross, and beyond where the cross streets had no names.

The sun grew hotter and we mopped our brows and sweated, but no one dropped out of the line. We passed Fairfield and headed into what the city dwellers considered to be real country, past the fork and the Do-Duck-Inn and the small pond that Mama and Papa called the Rice's pond. Finally, we turned the corner at our lane and headed toward our ten acres.

Next to our house on the south side was a giant excavation that had been dug out during the days of the WPA before I was born; after the WPA ended, the hole was left unfilled and since had grown up with blackberry vines, weeds, small plum trees, and various other low-growing brush. The white neighbor children and I frequently played on the "cliffs" and foraged in the trash piles that sundry people made by dumping their weekly refuse.

The city children found the clay pit intriguing and despite warning to be careful were soon scrambling over the mounds of hard clay and trying to climb the red "cliffs." Many, unused to the running blackberry vines, lacerated their legs as they ripped through the vines, not paying heed to which way their feet were going to where the vines were running.

The teachers would not let the children go to the creek, the best part of the whole place, and I was visibly disappointed. A few of us stole away despite the warnings and ventured to the edge of the water, some sticking their feet in, but hastily withdrawing them from the icy shock.

Finally, after the children ate whatever lunches they had brought, the teachers tried to round up the group, still busy chasing whatever chickens they had not already frightened into hiding. They lined up and waved goodbye to me as they took off on their long walk back to school.

During sixth grade the trip was repeated. The teachers evidently did not feel they could survive another hike, for they chartered a bus from the city transit authority and hauled us out in the bus, which was not nearly as much fun, especially for me, who rode the city busses to school and back every day.

Many times, usually alone, but sometimes accompanied by Jennie and Chessie when they grew a bit older, I would venture down the hill— beginning around March when the first violets appeared in the woods. There were several directions one could take. Sometimes I ventured out from the south side of the top two acres, heading down through the claypit that bordered our land and up onto a rounded hill. I would peer under each tree on one side of a path that wound down to the creek, looking for violets. To the untrained eye, I suppose there was little to see, but to one accustomed to trekking the woods, an adventure could almost always be had—and myriad treasures found—the violets in March and other wildflowers in other seasons. A bird's nest with two blue speckled eggs, maybe. I would peer in, delighting in the find. If the mother bird discovered me, she would sometimes make flying passes at my head until I scrambled away. Once in a great while I discovered baby birds, their mouths gaping wide for food. Sometimes there would be the abandoned shell of a locust left clinging to a tree, and other fascinating treasures.

Sometimes I would work my way down the hill on one side; at other times I crisscrossed from one side to the other. Once at the bottom of the hill, at least three choices presented themselves.

Straight ahead, I could wade or paddle about the creek itself, enjoying the water lilies that floated on the periphery—try to catch some of the thousands of minnows that darted about, sometimes hanging motionless in a vertical position, sometimes treading the water horizontally, then flitting off in an unexpected direction. If I had brought Mama's strainer, I would plunge it into the water and delight if I had actually succeeded in scooping a few of the swift creatures up to be deposited in a waiting jar filled with water. There were the tadpoles to be captured, taken home and watched. Often bright flowering plants grew around the water's edge at the point where trees grew, and many a time I longed to wade into the thickest part to pick the bright red or yellow or creamy white blossoms, but Mama and Grandma's warning of moccasins kept me on shore.

Sometimes I walked the worn path that meandered the full length of the creek. One time turning right, heading toward the wooden bridge, and at other times, turning left and following the path past the spring, the family's water supply before we had a pump.

The spring was surrounded by grass, bushes, and trees, and Mama and Grandma would dip their buckets in and bring up the clear, cold water that they hauled up the hill to the house. I was afraid to linger in the tall grasses too long for fear of being bitten by the snakes the two had warned of.

Often I would continue past the spring, heading north. It was cool, and I felt the wildness of the place all around me—the tall trees growing silently along the creek. Walking the road, I felt dwarfed. Whiffs of the wet marshy bog that began just off the path invaded my senses as I made my solitary way along the path, going nowhere in particular. Occasionally I would yell out "hello." The echo would come bouncing back from beyond the tree tops HELLO Hello hello.

Mama, Grandma, and Papa had often warned me about walking alone through the woods. They feared I would be accosted by hobos or mean-spirited types, so my senses were on alert, and if I ever spied men or boys or heard human voices I could not account for, I would scoot off the path and wait until what I perceived as danger had passed.

Often I was rewarded on these hikes by catching a glimpse of a rabbit bounding through the brush or finding a turtle creeping along. Once I found a mother dog and a litter of puppies nestled in a gully and worried Mama to let me go back and bring one of the puppies home. She insisted that the dog would turn vicious if its pups were disturbed. Later, when I went back for a second look, mother and pups were gone.

Cows, out to pasture, often walked about in the woods closer to the house, and I would watch these benign creatures methodically snipping off grass or contentedly chewing their cuds.

Sometimes I would sit in a clear spot in the middle of nowhere and breathe in the fresh air, gaze upward at the sky and become one with the place, motionless, watching the slight stirrings of a breeze and smelling the spicy aromas of varied grasses. Tiring, I would stretch out on the warm grass, birds in the surrounding trees resuming their cries and songs oblivious of an intruder.

Bull and the White Dog

Mama and I sometimes walked to a small store operated by an elderly couple. The store was called "Dad's" and was located on the corner of Davis Highway and the unnamed road that ran east to the clay pit that bounded the southernmost side of our land on a footpath that ran past our house and to the left until it crossed the black-topped road leading to Davis.

Usually, around seven or eight o'clock at night, Mama discovered that she was out of something that she needed to fix breakfast the following morning, and the two of us would set out for Dad's. About this time of night in the late fall, it would be pitch black outside, and as we walked to the path Mama almost invariably said that her hair was standing on end when we got about midway down the road to the blacktop. At Mama's words, my neck began to prickle, and sometimes if our dog, Bull, had followed along, his hair bristled, and he would growl at something in the woods on one side or the other. I could tell Bull's hair was bristling because he was a white dog with two black spots, and though the night was dark, the stars shone so brightly that I could see him indistinctly in the star shine.

I breathed a sigh of relief when we got off the path onto the blacktop and headed up the road. A few widely spaced houses stood on either side of the blacktop, and their electric lights glowing in the dark were comforting.

Usually Mama carried a long stick to beat away any bad dogs that might be on the road. That night, with Bull sniffing along, we set out for Dad's. Bull was a thick, heavy-set middle-aged dog who at certain times of the year was prone to getting into fights with other dogs who roamed the countryside at will.

When we reached Dad's that night, a shaggy white dog was lying outside waiting for someone who was buying something in the store. Bull growled; the white dog snarled. I never knew which dog made the first move, but they tangled just at the moment Mama opened the door to Dad's.

The store was tiny, just large enough to contain a counter on one side with items for sale stacked behind and other goods displayed on the opposite wall and to the back.

Mama opened the door and trying to follow, I was almost unbalanced by the two dogs who rushed pell-mell into the cramped space, snarling, snapping, and biting. The dogs rolled around on the floor. Dad yelled in his German accent, and his wife tried to rush in from the rear.

For an interminable time, teeth, fur, and fangs blurred. Mama still had the stick, and she commenced to stab and beat at the dogs. The blows raining down on the dogs only served to enrage them further. They fought their way down the length of the store and somehow managed to get behind the counter where we could determine the intensity and precise location of the battle by Dad's frenzied leaps as he tried to avoid being the unintended victim of their wrath.

Cans on the shelf behind the counter started to teeter and then to topple down on Dad's head as he did his impromptu dance trying to dodge the heavy cans from above and the snapping teeth below.

Someone (probably the other customer and owner of the white, shaggy dog) had enough presence of mind to open the front door, and finally the dogs tumbled out. Somehow we managed to buy whatever it was we needed, and Mama and I set out down the blacktop. Both dogs had vanished into the night.

The next day Bull turned up, looking rather subdued and bearing the scars of the previous night's battle. I painted his wounds with mercurochrome, the bright orange a strange contrast to his yellowed-white hair.

Wade in the Water

Early in the morning the women would gather buckets and lye soap and go down the hill to the creek. The water was clear and cold and deep, and the creek returned garments cleansed of yesterday's dust. The children would splash in that stream, and they too were cleansed, faces glistening in the early light. Some Sunday mornings the sisters and brothers from New Hope Baptist church would gather on the banks, and the preacher with a new concert would wade in.

This Sunday morning Grandma had already got up, put on her best clothes, and gone to the church. She had promised me that I could go to the baptizing at the creek later in the day.

After church, the congregation began to arrive. They came driving ancient cars, parking them around our yard or on the road in front, each car filled to overflowing. They picked their way along several barely visible paths. The women held up their skirts to prevent burrs and several varieties of clinging seeds from clutching their Sunday clothes.

Often, at other times when I did not go to the baptizing, I would listen at the top of the hill, ears straining, and presently the sounds of singing and moaning echoed up from the foot of the hill---sometimes loud and clear, sometimes waxing and waning.

Today I would get to go down the hill and witness the entire ritual. I tripped along the familiar path and soon stood with the crowd that had gathered at the edge of the water.

Young white youths and girls had abruptly ended their afternoon swim and stood in a respectful attitude somewhat removed from the dark horde that had gathered.

The converts fidgeted about, a bevy of young boys and girls in long, thin white garments with white towels wound around their heads. There were several larger adult versions of the children in the same white ensembles.

The preacher and deacons made unhurried final preparations. A deacon waded into the water and stabbed down a long, thin stick that protruded up out of the water. The preacher prepared to wade in. Soon he strode in as dignified a manner as possible out to the stake standing in the water and positioned himself waist-deep by its side. A deacon or sister raised a hymn.

They sang the first hymn and then offered a prayer:

"Lawd, it's once mo an' agin' dat we meet on the sho uf Jurden."

"A-men."

"Lawd, we bring dese humble souls to thee tuh be washed in the blood uh de lamb."

The prayer rolled out---solemn and earnest.

"An when we don wit dis sinful world, when we don shed the las tear, 'n prayed the last prayer; when we clos our eyes fuh de las time, I ast you to prepare a home for us in yo kingdom, where we live in peace fuhever mo. Amen."

"A-men. Yes. Jesus."

Grandma's strong voice raised the baptismal hymn as a deacon slowly guided the first repentant child out into the water.

"Take me to the wa-duh
Take me to the wa-duh
Take me to the wa-duh
Tuh be baptized."

Soulfully, the congregation hummed the melody.

The young sinner was relinquished into the hands of the preacher who folded the child's hands and placed them across his chest. Gripping the child with his own hand, covering the smaller ones and placing his other hand beneath the shoulder blades, the preacher intoned, "I baptize thee in de name of de fatha, de son, and de holy gos," and swiftly the young convert was dipped backward into the water, coming up sputtering and spitting out water.

"None but the righteous
None but the righteous
None but the righteous
Shall see Gawd."

The youngster was guided out of the water, the white gown drenched now and clinging to the thin body. A waiting sister's dark hands wrapped him in a dry towel, and the next convert was guided in.

"Wade in the wa-duh

Wade in the wa-duh, children
Wade in the wa-duh
Gawd's going tuh trouble the wa-duh."
When the last convert had been dipped, the
joyous song of celebration rang out:
Free at las
Free at las
Thang Gawd a'mighty
I'm free at las
Satan's chains had me bound
Thang Gawd a'mighty
I'm free at las
Free at las
Free at las
Thang Gawd a'mighty
I'm free at las
Been to the wa-duh and been baptized
Thang Gawd a'mighty I'm free at las
Free at las
Free at las
Thang Gawd a'mighty
I'm free at las

The Do

I got my hair "done" only twice a year---for Christmas and Easter. The first time I got my hair done I was six years old. Doris took me to her regular beauty parlor, but my hair was done, not by her regular beautician, but by another operator in the shop. After a while my hair began to come out in handfuls, and Mama and Grandma carried on for months about how the hairdresser had burned all my hair out. I had a thick crop of hair, and actually I couldn't miss the hair that came out in the comb when Doris or Mama got around to combing it. Still, I had recurring nightmares that all of my hair had fallen out, and I expected it to be lying on the pillow when I awakened.

Later on, after Doris married and went to New York, Mama took me to Mrs. Genevieve Nelson who kept a shop upstairs in a building owned by a dentist who had his office at the same location. It is the times I went to Mrs. Nelson's shop that I recall most vividly.

After I grew old enough to find my way around, I would go to Mrs. Nelson's shop by bus. I walked up the steep flight of stairs and entered the waiting room which extended down the full length of the area that was reserved for the shop. The operators had their booths extending down the full length of the shop on the other side of the wall that divided the two parts.

Usually I sat in the outer waiting room reading a book. Often it was a long wait. Sometimes Mrs. Nelson had to go down the street to her house to cook before she resumed her hairdresser role. Finally, Mrs. Nelson would call me, speaking a few words which I answered in monosyllables. She placed me in a chair in front of the shampoo bowl. I leaned back with my head in a sort of tray that sloped into the bowl. Mrs. Nelson lathered up my hair and rinsed it out several times.

When she had finished, the real agony began. When wet, my hair curled into loose springy spirals that were impossible to comb out. Nevertheless, she proceeded. Using a stout black comb, she worked her way through my hair. As long as the hair was wet, the combing proceeded with only minor discomfort for me. But the hair dried rapidly and before Mrs. Nelson had worked her way through my entire mop, most of the hair was dry. Dried, my hair was stiff and wiry. The comb would not move and Mrs. Nelson pulled and yanked the comb through as water puddled in my eyes. Usually as she untangled each section, she would twist it into a knot and pin it with a bobby pin so that it would not become snarled with the uncombed sections.

Finally, my hair was more or less combed out, and she unrolled all of the knots, combed through the entire mess and popped me under the dryer.

After the dryer, my hair was stiffer and wirier than ever. At last I was beckoned to the CHAIR. Mrs. Nelson sat propped on a high stool. On a table were assorted jars of grease. An open jar would have particles of burnt or broken hair caught in the viscous jelly. The straightening comb rested on some kind of burner, smoking from grease on its surface. Mrs. Nelson took a comb and parted off small sections, applying a generous amount of grease to the hair near the scalp. Then, taking the heavy curved hot iron, she proceeded to pull the teeth through the small section of hair. The grease sizzled as it made contact with the hot comb and smoke rose as the comb was pulled through the grease, frying the hair and straightening it as it proceeded. Mrs. Nelson used a cloth each time she pulled the comb through the hair to absorb excess grease. Sometimes untouched snarls formed a knot at the end of the hair, and she would force the comb through, breaking off the end of the hair.

She placed the comb back on the burner and hair caught in its teeth crackled and burned, and the shop was always filled with the acrid smell of burning hair, mixed with the smell of hot, perfumed grease.

For what seemed like hours, Mrs. Nelson sectioned off the hair and pulled the comb through. This process was usually painful, for I was "tender-headed" and the rough comb raking through my roughened hair was excruciating. Often the hot grease seeped down onto the scalp.

Doing the edges was most terrifying of all. Mrs. Nelson took a straight-toothed hot comb and came paralyzingly close to the skin on my face at the hairline. Occasionally the comb touched the skin; it was especially perilous at the ears. Around my head she went, as the hair, now greasy and straight would be pressed further. Now the small comb at the scalp no longer lay between my scalp, and she brought the hot comb dangerously close to the scalp to straighten the kinks that had escaped beneath the barrier comb.

After she had straightened the hair, the process of sectioning the hair was repeated. This time she applied the curling iron, and for another long while I could hear the click-click-click of the iron as she fashioned the "do." After an eternity, I was given the mirror to look at my crowning mass of grease-soaked curls.

Throughout the process I grimaced in silence, reading a book, occasionally being yanked when, absorbed in some fantasy, I failed to hold my head just so. My scalp was usually sore for several days.

Despite the smell of burning hair in the shop, Mrs. Nelson was actually a skilled operator, and my hair remained long and luxuriant until I cut it off when I was fifteen. Many girls' hair diminished with the years, becoming short and stubby from continuous straightening by unskilled operators.

Fish Head Soup and Sassafras Tea

Mama created nourishing meals using everything that was edible. When we ate chicken on Sundays or sometimes on weekdays, every part, except the entrails was consumed.

The chicken's head was severed on the chopping block or its neck was snapped by a few deft twists. The fowl fluttered helplessly in the yard briefly, and when the tremors subsided, it was placed in a pan and was doused with scalding water, loosening the feathers which were then plucked.

I was partial to wings, while Mama consumed the back. The chicken was fried in a pan or smothered in onions and gravy or boiled in a pot. I also favored the feet and the head. The feet and heads were fried and rendered hard and crisp. I cracked open the head and drew out the succulent brain. Sometimes the feet and other bony parts were combined with the giblets and stewed or made into soups and eaten with rice.

Another soup Mama made that was a special treat was a concoction made from the heads of red snapper. Mama claimed that snapper cost too much to eat on a regular basis, so she bought the cheaper mullet to fry. She would ask the owner of the fish market or an attendant to throw in a couple of snapper heads. These she would boil in water with diced onions and a couple of tablespoons of flour for thickening and salt and pepper seasoning. The result was simple but tasty.

Sometimes Mama would command, "Go get the shovel, Baby." I scampered away and returned dragging the shovel while Mama gathered up the hatchet and a brown paper sack. We went out behind the house and down to the back of Grandma's chicken yard to dig for sassafras roots.

It was time for sassafras tea---it was always time for tea around October when the first nip tingled the air and the sap was down. The migrating birds had already flown south a month or more ago, and winter was coming on.

Mama took the hatchet and hacked down a medium-sized tree. Then she dug into the rich black dirt and drew out the pungent-smelling roots. They were light ivory inside but covered with dirt. She chopped the roots of several trees into small pieces just large enough to fit into the old battered coffee pot she kept especially for brewing the tea.

Every evening, just before bedtime, we would drink a steaming cup of the brew. Its smell circulated throughout the house and drew us like blow flies to collard greens and is always associated in my mind with approaching winter on the Gulf Coast and of coziness, warmth and well-being.

The reddish liquid was mixed with a teaspoon or so of sugar, and we sipped our cupfuls, often returning until the pot was dry. The tea was supposed to ward off all manner of ills and fortify one's blood and system for the rigors of a harsh winter. Unlike some of the more unpalatable tonics and purges, (castor oil, black draught), sassafras tea was not one that caused frowns and rebellions. It was hot and spicy and sweet, and we relished it.

Doris said before I was born, Mama made fresh hog head cheese from the head of a hog, the feet, ears and snout. These she boiled together and squeezed through cheese cloth, adding spices and a generous quantity of vinegar.

If there were no lemons to make lemonade or tea for iced tea, she made a sweetened beverage by pouring a hefty quantity of cane syrup into water and adding ice.

There was always a variety of vegetables: collard and turnip greens in fall and winter eaten with crackling bread made from pork cracklins and baked sweet potatoes.

In summer there were snap beans, black-eyed peas, butter beans, tomatoes, squash and okra, all home grown.

We normally did not eat wild animals since no one hunted these creatures. Rabbits and squirrels and birds were left alone, but once a possum that was raiding the hen house served as a meal.

Around eight or nine o'clock the chickens in Grandma's chicken yard began to raise a ruckus, cackling and fluttering about in distress. "Better go see what's wrong wit them chickens," Papa said. We waited a while and presently Papa came back with a possum. "He's a fat 'um," Grandma said, "Make good eatin'."

The possum was killed, singed and dressed. The next day, Mama cooked the scoundrel, surrounding him with baked sweet potatoes, and I had my first taste of a wild creature from the woods.

Often we made meals of greens and cornbread or dried black-eyed peas and cornbread. These meals I was inclined to skip, never having developed a lusty appetite for boiled vegetables.

The most scrumptious meals were served on Christmas day. Before my Aunt Doris left to live in New York, Mama and Doris baked fruit cakes and pies into the nights leading up to Christmas. The tantalizing aromas filtered through the house and floated on air currents to the neighboring lanes and streets.

The Saturday before Christmas, Papa and I would make our way down the hill into the woods and search for a short-leaf pine. We would find a tree, look it over and move on until we finally found one to our liking. Papa cut the tree down with the ax and brought it home on his shoulder.

I would take down the carefully wrapped ornaments of delicately colored shells and round silver balls that Doris had bought before going to New York. I would decorate the tree and admire my creation at night, watching the flames from the fire in the fireplace reflected in the silver ornaments or gaze at my distorted reflection in the mirror-like shells.

Christmas eve was given over entirely to cooking. Mama would let me chop celery, bell pepper and onions for potato salad. I chopped the onion, wiping away the tears brought on by the stinging juice.

Mama had usually baked the two cakes that were the crowning accomplishment of her Christmas labors. A ten-egg yolk pound cake, and a white coconut cake made from the ten egg whites. The cakes had usually been baked several days before Christmas, and Christmas eve night I would tackle the coconut, scraping my knuckles on the tin grater until blood sometimes trickled into the grated coconut.

We made fruit salad from every conceivable kind of fruit and nuts and tossed it with mayonnaise.

Mama had par-boiled a large hen on Christmas eve and on Christmas morning made cornbread dressing and baked the hen and dressing in the oven of the wood stove.

Usually I had a churning stomach on Christmas eve from drinking unbelievable combinations of juices drained from canned fruits---pineapple, fruit cocktail, cherry---and licking icing bowls and snitching tiny pieces of coconut too small to grate, not to mention halves of bananas, handfuls of pecans, diced apples and sections of oranges.

I crawled into bed anticipating Santa's arrival. Mama left the front door ajar, for I had concluded that there was no way Santa would come down our black, sooty chimney hauling a bag of toys later in the night.

Rodeo

When I was around nine or ten years old, my life was a solitary one. Most of the fun I had I still created for myself. Occasionally, neighbor white children and I played on the clay banks of the giant excavation that had been dug out following the Depression as a WPA project. I spent the summer reading, swinging in my make-shift swing, going to the creek for an occasional dip or daydreaming.

Then for one glorious summer everything changed. There was something new and exciting in the air. It all began with the arrival of Jody.

Jody was a white man in his early fifties, a stocky build and a gruff demeanor. He had come from out west somewhere, and when he arrived in Pensacola following his wife and step-daughter, he found Pensacola's sleepy atmosphere decidedly too tame. Apparently his past had been filled with the stuff of legends---the wild and untamed west was in his blood.

Before a month had passed, Jody had hit upon the idea of starting a rodeo---in Pensacola. I probably never would have known about this grand venture, but the daughter-in-law was married to one of our neighbors, and the rodeo was to take place right in front of our front porch.

Across the dirt road that later became Lynell Street was the Garrison property. It extended in a straight line down the expanse of our front property line to Fiftieth Street. Adjacent to the Garrison property was another rectangular swatch of land that had been bought by one of the Powell sons but had not been developed. This plot was clearly visible from my front porch, and it was here that Jody decreed the rodeo would open.

Over a period of a month, Jody repaired the wire fence, built bleachers on the property and brought in horses, calves, bulls, and a few rangy-looking cowboy types.

Then one Saturday afternoon the bleachers began to fill with spectators and the show was on.

Now I knew a little something about roping calves and twirling lassoes from the Saturday matinees that I consumed. Westerns had never been my favorite celluloid entertainment---I preferred musicals, but I had seen Randolph Scott and Gary Cooper ride off into many a sunset.

Papa, Mama, Grandma and I all gathered on the porch, the grownups providing a running commentary on what was transpiring across the fence.

"Look at that fool," Papa said. "He go bust hisself wide open."

"Look at that thing buck," Mama chimed in.

"Lawd, he sho kin twirl that thing. Looka there."

Various whoops and hollers and yippees came floating our way.

The adults watched for a while, but soon chores called, and I was left, mesmerized by the whole display.

Well, this went on for most of the summer. Then rumors began to circulate about Jody. Mama, who was always on top of neighborhood gossip, heard that something was going on between Jody and the Johnson's new daughter-in-law.

"I heard that that Jody and that Luseen 'oman been messin' around long fore they come down heah," Mama said.

Well, that rodeo and all its frontier atmosphere came to a grand halt on Saturday night. After the rodeo, round about eight o'clock, there rose up a big commotion. Shouts and yells and cussing came our way as we sat on the front porch.

"What in the world?" Mama said. Usually it was so quiet out our way that the only sounds were crickets and sometimes frogs down on the creek. You could literally gear the corn grow. Once in a while you could hear a low guttural sound that Mama and Papa said was an alligator.

After a few days, Mama was able to piece together what happened. After Jody appeared with a large white bandage wound around his head, Mama "heard" that Mr. J., Lousene's father-in-law, had gotten into a fight with Jody, telling him to leave Lousene alone. Then he had laid a baseball bat upside Jody's head, splitting his head wide open and causing a gash that needed twenty-five stitches.

Anyway, right after the big fight, the horses and calves and cowboys left and the rodeo closed.

Jody went back to Texas or wherever he had ridden in from, and I was back to daydreaming.

Moving On

In 1947, when I entered seventh grade at Washing ton High school, the only black high school in the county, I was a skinny girl with thick braids and thin knobby knees. I was an inquisitive child who pursued a restless search for knowledge through whatever mean I could find. The battery-powered radio---a gift to Doris from a boyfriend before she moved to New York took me beyond the small, sleepy Gulf coast town of Pensacola. Movies gave me a glimpse of the glamour of Hollywood, and comic books and fan magazines satisfied my craving for excitement. The great writers of my aunt's and uncle's ol English and American literature anthologies opened the world of literature and ideas to me.

From the radio I had been learning since my fourth or fifth year of the events and times to which I had been born. Along with Papa, I listened attentively to the world news as it crackled in from London and Paris. During the war it was Edward R. Murrow, and on Sunday nights the staccato delivery of Walter Winchell. Throughout the week comedy and soap operas, mystery and opera on Saturday afternoon, popular music from the <u>Hit Parade</u> and the <u>Grand Ole Opry</u> from Nashville---all had informed my growing sensibility.

When I tired of the radio's babble and escaping into the marvelous adventures of comic book heroes and heroines like Wonder Woman, Batman, and Superman and the pulp stories in the romance magazines I had taken to buying along with the comic books from the newsstand on Palafox Street. I wandered the family's ten acres and the surrounding countryside, and intimate acquaintance of wild flowers and insects, frogs and minnows, buttercups, violets, and the tiny white flowers of nettles. I knew the wide slick leaves of jimson weed and other sundry flora that grew wild in the woods beyond the cleared space that was the yard and playground and had been the site of my dollhouse when I was five or six.

Mama would rather do most of the household duties herself. Grandma gave me a generous supply of tips from her nightly labors at the tourist camp, and I was left to my own devices--to fill the hours when school was out as I chose, doing whatever work my whimsy led me to.

In late August, Mama took me to the high school on the opposite side of town before school started, and a few teachers marveled at the A's on my sixth grade report card, each expressing a desire to have me as a student.

Washington High School was a far cry from Spencer Bibbs where Mrs. Pickens had known all of us by name and I had known most of my classmates. Washington High School drew students from the eight black grade schools in the county. At first the mass of students was overwhelming. Strange, wild young creatures from parts of town I had never ventured into came together in a school equipped and supplied with used materials from Pensacola High, the largest white school in the county.

For most of seventh grade I existed on the periphery of school life. I dutifully completed homework assignments and my grades were high. I made one lasting friend, a deep brown-skinned girl with outrageously bowed legs and wide mischievous dark eyes. Lena lived on the extreme opposite end of the county, so mostly our friendship was confined to school hours. Lena was loud of speech and laughter, bursting into shrill, piercing spasms of uncontrollable merriment at the slightest provocation. Lena's vocabulary was sprinkled with epithets that I had never heard, foul language being unheard of in my life with Papa, Mama, and Grandma.

Lena was a reader too, and together we discovered the racy, earthy novels of Erskine Caldwell. During the year we read and giggled our way through God's Little Acre, Tragic Ground, and Tobacco Road. These I hid from Mama who was too much caught up in work to pay close attention to my eclectic collection of reading material.

At school Lena and I spent lunch hour and the time before school took in escaping the advances of mannish boys who threatened to drag us into the basement to do "it." Often Lena would join the boys and shove me into the gross creatures who would plant a wet kiss on my cheek as I snatched my mouth away in disgust.

Lena and I parted company when the bell rang at the end of the day, and Lena climbed into the school bus and I waited for the city transportation to another bus to the north end where my family's ten acres were located.

In the spring the man Grandma worked for at the cabins wanted space to keep additional bees. We had always kept six or seven rotting hives of our own. The new bees were a diversion. I found out all I could about the creatures and stood observing as Mr. Jack brought the compact white painted hives and placed them at five or six locations behind Grandma's chicken yard. Inside the hives were racks made of new wood. Mr. Jack explained how the bees make the waxy combs and in the fall they would be filled with light amber colored honey. I knew that the queen bee's sole purpose was to be fertilized by the drones and to lay eggs which turned into larvae and emerged sometime later as the winged busy creatures who ceaselessly sought the pollen of honeysuckle vines and Mama's bright flowers. After fertilization, the queen would kill the hapless drones.

When the bees swarmed, Mr. Jack donned netting that covered his face, plied the bees with smoke, and I watched in amazement as the insects crawled harmlessly over his hands and arms. When the bees swarmed, the giant swarm was gathered in a buzzing, crawling mass and deposited in the hive that was to be their home and which they would return to after numerous pollen-gathering forays.

The space below the chicken yard had to be cleared of downed trees and branches from the hurricane that struck the county in September. I remembered the storm with a thrill mixed with the fear I had felt as we had ridden it out in our fragile house. School had let out early and when I came home, the clouds had begun to race across the sky, driven by swift gusts of wind. The usually clean-swept yard had begun to accumulate twigs and small branches that snapped when the thick leaves were convulsed in the wind.

The winds gradually increased, soon gusting at about forty miles per hour. Now the rain began to pelt the trees, shrubs, and earth. The rain came in brief scattered bursts, and the wind made a rushing noise as it smote the trees. More small twigs and leaves snapped and the ground was becoming more littered.

Night came on and the winds continued to increase.

Grandma was working at a tourist came that night. The camp was located about six blocks from where we lived and Grandma walked there in the early evening and returned early in the morning.

All through that terrifying night, the storm raged. We huddled together, lest the violent winds rip the frail and ancient house apart. The huge chinaberry trees snapped at the bases and crashed to the ground. Leaks had sprung in the rotten shingles of the roof, and as it became increasing ly more difficult to find a dry spot, we prayed to be spared. The old house was stronger than we thought, and at daybreak still stood more or less intact, but the winds still raged.

Rainy Day

In the shadowy light furnished by the kerosene lamp, Mama and Papa themselves moved like shadows. Mama yanked the sheets from the iron bed with its peeling white paint; she upended the top mattress of black and white striped ticking, its contents spilling onto the floor's bare splintery boards. Getting down to the bottom mattress, she ripped the seams and stirred around in lumpy cotton, pulling out fistfuls of ten and twenty dollar bills. I stood, my mouth open, in amazement.

I had always thought that we were poor, and indeed we were, or certainly lived like it.

Mama glanced at me. "Don't be talking 'bout this to <u>nobody,</u> y'hear? This is for a rainy day. Don't never talk family business to <u>nobody.</u>" I had heard it before and kept the family secrets locked inside---in the sanctity of mind, unfettered and free only in dreams.

They drifted from the disheveled bed outside into the sultry darkness, the lamp sending grotesque shadows advancing toward the chicken yard. We paused at the makeshift pen that housed the chickens, Papa removing the metal sheet from the top. The fowl huddled together, turning glassy, sleepy eyes toward the intrusive light. Papa removed a board, scraping away droppings and dug into the earth beneath. The light from the lamp fell on something that Papa pulled from the ground. He continued to dig. Soon, the light revealed a row of mason jars with dusty lids. In the jars, rolls of money lay sealed in airtight vacuums.

In the days that followed Mama told me the story of the buried treasure. It was ours. We had robbed no banks nor burgled no houses. The money had been scrimped and saved for thirty years. Mama raised chickens and Papa hauled eggs to work and sold them by the dozen to fellow workers. Charging interest, Papa lent money to men at work, men who lived for the moment and were broke on Monday morning. Illegal, no doubt. Papa made a garden; Mama sold the fresh vegetables to whoever sought them. Mama washed and ironed and cleaned houses. Penny by penny they saved a tidy nest-egg.

They had scrimped and saved the money for thirty years, and following the Depression, not trusting the banks, black Marners, they had stuffed it in mattresses and buried it under the dusty floor of the chicken coup. The children had gone uneducated, a decent home unbuilt. They allowed themselves only the luxury of adequate food. Following the scene I witnessed, Mama hauled the molding bills to the Florida National Bank. It was for that distant rainy day.

A son, languishing in the Florida backwaters, died at the hands of a lynch mob, unable to muster the cash to pursue the dream of a college education. Two children migrated to eastern cities to escape the grips of poverty. One died in a Christmas day crash when the ancient car in which she was riding crashed into an unlighted truck beside the road. She was my mother. Finally, Papa himself died.

I escaped on scholarship money gained through competitive examination. One fall in the early sixties living in another city, I bought the hometown paper and a short article caught my eye:

"ELDERLY WOMAN VICTIM OF FLIM FLAM"

I read the story. The elderly woman was Mama. In the ensuing years, she grew suspicious of even those closest to her. She saved most of her Social Security check as I paid for necessities. She was still saving for a rainy day.

Grandma

Grandma was a woman of action. Mama stayed home and did the household drudgery, but Grandma was out in the world, at least during the last years of her life. While they both took in washing and ironing, Grandma was not a slave to it; she polished off her bundle and was off to more interesting things. By the time I was old enough to be aware of Grandma, she was legendary. Mama said when she was younger, she could plow like a man and shoot like a marksman. It was Grandma who took me away from our ten acres on a regular basis. She would be off to see various important folks around town, and invited me to come along.

"Com on 'n go wit Gramma down town," and we would be off.

I remember going to Dr. Stokes's office, following Grandma to some sort of "business" engagement. The memory that lingers from that outing was seeing a baby boy just after circumcision. I heard the squalling protestations from the wounded mite before I saw him. His screams hit like assault waves as we entered the building. Walking down a hall, I glanced through an open door. The baby lay on a table, his face contorted with pain and aggrievement. The entire lower part of his trunk, including his penis, was a bloody mess. The bright red blood burned its impression on my brain. I didn't know what had

happened, but prayed that I should never be
forced to endure it.

Some of Grandma's experiences were
amusingly recollected by Mama or Doris.

"Remember the time Grandma went up to
Clopton's and they got her drunk?"

"Lawd, Mama come back staggering and
talkin' outta her head. Went right to bed and was
sleep before a cat could lick his paw."

"Remember the time Grandma couldn't get
no ride home from the church? Grandma, she'd
ride in anybody's old piece 'a car, but anyhow, we
looked down the road and here come Brother
Johnson and Grandma ridin' on his bicycle. Come
all the way from Goulden ridin' on dat bicycle.
Grama musta been seventy-five year old."

"Gramma was sum-pn. Begged the white
folks for money all over dis county to build that
church. She'd walk up to some white man, say,
'Son, woncha gimme fifty cents, hep bill us a
church?' White man reach in his pocket, pull out a
dollar bill. Church 'uz meetin' under a bush arbor;
raised enough money to build a real buildin'.'"

Grandma became the Mother of New Hope
Baptist Church and relished the intrigue of church
politics. When I went to church with her, she
prayed the longest and the loudest prayers. Her
voice was strong and ringing, and must have been
audible to the inhabitants of paradise. She was in
charge of baking the communion bread and
bringing the grape juice to church every first
Sunday. The tiny communion glasses were stored

in her washstand during the rest of the month. I
liked to snitch pieces of the bland, hard bread, and
a swig of the grape juice was indeed as close to
heaven as I cared to come.

Grandma and I were together a lot. I loved
to comb her short, curly salt and pepper hair. It
was soft and full, and I never learned why it had
changed from the abundant crop she sported in an
old formal photograph to the mannish cut it was
when I knew her.

I was still a little embarrassed by the way
Grandma dressed. She wore long, flowing skirts
that Mrs. Creighton made from fabric Grandma
bought at Porter's Bazaar. Nobody else wore
dresses quite like Grandma's, and I wondered why
she clung to her own old-fashioned style. Certainly
it was a distinguishing one.

Grandma would stand up to anybody. She
feared no man nor no thing. When we went to the
creek, boys who might be swimming scrambled
out of the water while we washed out clothes,
Grandma defying them to reenter. The whites
called her "Aunt Jenny," a source of constant
irritation to Doris and Mama, and later to me. The
creek crossing her land came to be called Jenny's
Hole, the communal pond where people swam in
the heat of summer and bathed on Saturday
nights. She had become a part of local myth.

One peculiarity of hers left the family
perplexed. She had managed to save almost a
thousand dollars from her pension and the job she
had at the tourist camp where she walked every

evening. She trusted the banks no more than
Mama and Papa did, but she let a white woman
friend keep her money for her. The money and the
woman's keeping it were the source of many
heated arguments. Somehow it would always
come up.

"Mama, I don' see how come you let that ole
woman keep yo money. Niggers always ruther
trust white folks then they own people. That ole
'oman go git all you money when you die."

"I do what I please wit my money."

"Sho is crazy. Don you know how many
niggers done loss they money and they property
to white folks?"

"Miz C. got plenty money. She don need my
little bit."

"That how she got it. Thas how they all get
it. Beat some po nigga outta his money."

"You ten' to you bidness; I ten' to mine."

Mama and Fred often told the story of how
Grandma got one white woman "tole."

It seems that a giant dog had come up out of
the woods. The dog hung about the house for days,
defying their attempts to chase it away. It
menaced passersby and had a vicious streak.

One night Fred had come home late, and
"Bob" as Grandma had named the dog because of
its cropped tail, lunged at Fred just as he
approached the gate. Fred took off running, taking
a flying leap for the porch, getting inside the house
as the dog's sharp teeth snapped at his heels.

After that incident, the family feared the dog. Grandma thought it was time to get rid of him. She ran an ad in the newspaper, and a few days later, a tall, thin woman with dirty blonde hair drove up in a late model car. The woman was stylishly dressed and appeared haughty and overbearing, unlike the neighboring whites who were generally good folks ready for a chat.

Grandma greeted the woman with a cordial "Howdy-do." The woman saw the dog, and ignoring Grandma, called out, "Bob." The dog came forward, but instead of walking to the woman, sat on its haunches by Grandma's side.

Grandma explained how the dog had come up out of the woods and how it had almost attacked Fred.

The woman's lips turned down, and she appeared not to believe Grandma's story, indicating that she believed the animal had been lured away and that she was upset over what she felt was an act of common thievery.

Grandma's hackles bean to rise. She glared at the woman:

"This dawd come up heah. We don' have no need for a dog like this. Is you crazy? We run the ad in the paper askin' for you to come git the dawg. If we tryin' to steal im, why we do that?" Grandma was getting hotter and hotter. "You know whut I thinks? I thinks you wuz out in the woods, up to some uf your foolishness with some man 'n the dog run off. Don' come heah a'cuzin' us of stealin' the dog, you nasty stinkin' huzzy. You take this dawg 'n git away from heah."

The most vivid memory of Grandma remains the time when she braved a hurricane to get home to "see 'bout my folks."

We had ridden out the terrifying storm all night. As day dawned, the old house had survived, but Grandma, away at the cabins, could not know. Around seven o'clock the winds still raged. We were socked in by downed trees. Hot wires were down and lying on the asphalt on Fiftieth Street. We figured Grandma would stay at camp until the storm let up and the roads were cleared. As the sky lightened, I recall peering out the door and beholding a sight that will always live as one of my most vivid recollections. Coming down the dirt road was Grandma, her long skirts billowing and whipped wildly out by the ferocious wind. She leaned a bit in those days anyway, but the force of the wind caused her to tilt even more. As the broom sedge and straw bowed and flattened and the branches of the still standing trees danced and vibrated as though possessed by demons, she strode with a determination born of years of pitting her will against the forces of the elements and of men. Each step impeded by the force of the wind, she made an awesome sight as she struggled against it, her head wrapped in a rain-soaked shawl, the ends of which flew fitfully back in the gale. Grandma was like that. She would take on a man, a woman, or a storm with equal determination.

In the summer before I entered ninth grade, Grandma fell ill. She was nearing eighty-five and had continued to work all night at the cabins, keep up with church functions, and other "business." One day when Mama suggested that she slow down, she said, "When death gets me, he'll hafta catch me. I won' be settin' heah waitin'."

Grandma had grown frail in recent days, and that summer when she could go no longer, she was taken to Sacred Heart Hospital. I continued going to movies once or twice a week. They kept the creeping dread away at least for a couple of hours.

When Grandma was brought home and taken from the ambulance on a stretcher, she looked fat and bloated. Her skin was paler and lighter than I remembered. She was placed on her bed, and except for getting up to eat and use the slop pot, she was confined there until November.

Grandma was a difficult patient. She had always exaggerated aches and pains, and now she cried out in her still loud and ringing voice,

"uhhhhh-Lawwwwwd; uhhhhhhhh Lawwwwwwwwwwwwd!"

Grandma's cries stabbed me like a knife. I was terrified that she would die, and prayed and played mental games to keep her alive.

In November, on Sunday just before Thanksgiving, Mama had tried to give Grandma some breakfast, but she had refused it. She had been eating little, but this morning, she refused nourishment entirely.

I heard her call
"Uhhhhhhhhhhhh, Sister."
Mama and I entered her room, my heart
beating dully. Grandma wheeled off the bed and
Mama steadied her to get the pot. Mama managed
to get Grandma back in bed. She lay on her back;
suddenly her eyes rolled toward the ceiling. I
heard a soft rattle.

Mama hovered over Grandma. Then she
covered her face, and stopping the clock, she
covered its face, too. I stood, utterly stunned.

Stories

When Grandma died, Uncle Fred came down for the funeral. Doris, who had visited in the summer, did not come.

Fred was now living in New York's Harlem. I had seen Fred only once before when I was around seven years old. He had come, dressed in his army uniform, a tall, slender, handsome young man. He was stationed at Fort Hachuncha, Arizona. I remember because of the silken pillow cover that he sent Mama that bore the name of the army post and rested on Doris's bed in Grandma's room.

I developed a decided distaste for Fred growing out of an incident that occurred during that visit. We had gathered for dinner, seated at the long table in the kitchen---Mama, Papa, Grandma, Doris, Fred, and me. The dinner was in progress with lively talk, Fred asking and answering questions about the war and the army. Fred directed a question to Grandma. Grandma started to answer. I said, "Naw, Grandma, that's not what happe---" Fred's arm shot out, and his flat open hand caught me full in the face, a stinging blow. Stunned, I blinked at Fred, then jumped up from the table and ran outside. Behind the kitchen, I wailed, sobbing in indignation. Doris ran after me; she cradled me in her arms, saying, "That's all right, Baby. Fred thought you were being

71

disrespectful to Grandma by interrupting her. Fred's not used to little children."

Afterward, I heard Mama telling Papa, "He oughtna hit the child. She don' know him; he ain' never been heah since she got bigger. Made me mad."

At any rate, when Fred came for Grandma's funeral, I was leery of him, still remembering the slap, one of the few I ever received. I was sure to watch my mouth. Fred seemed cordial, however, hugging and kissing me and asking, "Whas happenin'?"

The night before the funeral, the family talked late into the night, reliving family history, Some of the stories I had heard before. That night, though, the full impact of some of the stories first seemed to sink in, though they were repeated in one form or another throughout my life.

The talked of the death of my Uncle William, almost fifteen years earlier.

"William, he wuz smart. He coulda made somthin' 'a hisself. He could draw---still got some 'a the drawins he don 'a the human body. He wanted to be a scientist."

"Lawd, I 'member the night he got kilt. Those white folks, they kilt 'im cause 'a dat ole white gal up at the tourist came."

I 'member...

William had gone to a movie with Doris and Janie and some friends. Then he went to the creek- -the creek that ran across the lower part of our ten acres. The creek where the whole community

72

swam in the summer. Everybody gathered at the hole---swimming for recreation; others, further down the stream, taking their weekly bath on Saturday nights. William had gone there that night. Suddenly, he burst into the house, searching for something.

"What you lookin' fuh, boy?"

"Nothin."

"Whare you going'?"

"Never min', I be back."

William found what he was looking for a set off in a flash, heading out the south gate, going toward the highway through the woods.

Papa shook his head, feeling disquieted. Time congealed, but the usual nightly chores had to be done. Mama and the girls struggled with the nightly mess of dirty dishes and greasy pots and pans. William did not return. Papa worried. Suddenly he made a decision. He went toward the back of the room, looking for the gun. It was not in its usual hiding place. His heart beat ominously. "I'm going up the road."

Papa set out into the darkness, out the gate, then veering off, taking a footpath through the woods. It was early September, Labor Day. The leaves on the blackjacks on either side of the road were still green, but beginning to yellow and redden. In the darkness, their color was not visible, but they rustled softly as he brushed past.

Halfway up the path, he saw something lying in the road. He quickened his steps. Getting closer, he saw it was a body, lying face down on the path. He stooped over. The hands were tied behind the back. The clothes and form looked like William's, but Papa suspended reaction.

With his right hand, he turned the body over. It was William, a piece of cloth tied across his mouth. The gun lay on the path, opposite him.

"My Gawd, they shot 'im wit his own gun."

"The no good crackers. They killed 'im ova that ole gal."

"Lawd, them wuz dark days. First William; then Janie." Mama looked at me. "Ya'll almost tuk the baby. Almost tuk the baby. I said, 'Ya'll leve that baby, heah. Got no bidness takin' that baby out in the cole. Musta been the Lawd make me stop yuh fom takin' that baby."

My mother, Janie, and Doris had jumped into my father's car. It was Christmas day, 1936. I was one year old.

They had driven around, stopping here and there, taking a leisurely joy ride. The sun moved toward the western horizon and finally sank behind the trees. As darkness descended, they headed toward home so as not to anger Mama and Papa who worried when the children were out after dark. The car made its way onto Davis Highway, Doris, Janie and Bob laughing and talking. Suddenly, a deafening crash---the car had hit an unlighted truck beside the road.

Papa heard the crash. He said, "Somebody done had a accident." Curious, he set out walking, taking a shortcut through the woods. He came out of the woods near the turntable on Davis. He found the spot, fresh blood still coloring the road.

"Somebody died," he murmured. He shook his head, then walked back through the woods to the house. The children had not returned.

An hour or more passed. A car drove up into the yard. It was Joe Morris from the funeral home.

"Sim, Janie's dead. Doris is hurt in the hospital."

Papa felt his world stop for the second time in two years.

"Lawd," Mama said, patting me on the knee. "Almos tuk the baby."

American Dream

As I grew older, into pre-adolescence and adolescence, I agonized more and more over the shabbiness of my surroundings. After the revelation of Mama's and Papa's nest egg, it seemed incomprehensible to me why some portion of money could not be spent on improving the appearance of our physical surroundings. Certainly there seemed to be enough money to make some renovations if not build a new dwelling.

I balked at bringing my newly-found friends home. What would they think? Their surroundings, while not sumptuous, certainly gave a more pleasant impression.

"But, Mama, why can't we remodel the house? At least add a living room and put in a bathroom."

"This old place is too far gone. You want us to spend every penny we got? Take a lot 'a money to do this kind 'a thing. Better to build a whole new house."

"But, Mama, all the other children's houses look better than ours. I can't have any friends come home with me."

"These chi-run lak you for yo house? These ain' no real friends."

"But, Mama, they'll laugh and make fun of me."

"Whut diffrunce it make whut they say. You still you."

"Mama, my God."

"Don' be takin' the Lawd's name in vain. You watch yo mouth."

When I broached the subject to Papa he was noncommittal.

"Yo Mama and me---we see. Take a lot 'a money. This house do to live in. Shouldna never let you see we got no money. Don' be talkin' family bidness in the street. Folks come in heah, knock our heads off. Think we got money. You keep you mouf shet."

"But, Papa, couln't we just wall in the porch and make it a living room? And maybe cover the sides with asbestos siding? That would make a big difference."

"We see. Go on an' hep yo Mama. Stop worryin' folks to death."

I would give up for a while, meantime trying to devise ways to improve the appearance of the house. The outside was beyond hope. Grandma's room was the only possibility. I bought Rit and dyed the fragile Priscilla curtains a bright pink to complement the two chenille spreads. One was white with tiny pink and blue and yellow flowers. The other was a light salmon with white puffs woven over. Grandma's rug was beginning to be a bit frayed in spots, but was still presentable.

The room that Mama, Papa, and I inhabited was a disaster---two iron beds that were often unmade and an eclectic collection of odds and ends---a decrepit washstand where I studied at night by the light of the lamp or later under the naked electric light bulb that hung from a wire suspended from the ceiling. In one corner was a sort of bench that Papa had made that served as a bookcase and held my hundreds of comic books, and to the back of the room a screened in baby bed that I had slept in when I was first born, now filled with clutter. On the north end were two giant wooden chests that contained, in one, a tangled and knotted assortment of clothes not currently being worn, but constantly sifted through, and the other the folded quilts and spreads that Mama considered too good to use. Between these two chests a battered trunk stood, filled with assorted objects that I delighted in examining when nothing better presented itself for diversion.

At some point we had painted the walls in both Grandma's room and ours, but the paint and begun to mildew in spots. These two rooms were sealed, but the kitchen gave a view of exposed soot blackened rafters and was filled with the long table that remained from the once large family, the black wood stove, two safes, and various other eccentrically collected junk.

I constructed a thousand dreams and fantasies around re-modeling the house or building a new one; In my mind I knocked out walls, added partitions and furniture that surely we could never pay for. I would return to Mama and Papa, plaguing them at regular intervals.

Nothing seemed to have any effect. If they ever discussed the matter, it was long after I slept.

Sometimes if I could catch the two of them together, I would bring up the subject, my private obsession.

"Papa, couldn't we wall in the back porch too. Use the back porch for a dining room and bath and the front porch as a living room?"

This ol house ain' strong enough for that. The foundations is weak. Go to knockin' on this shack, it fall down on top of you.

"Well, let's build another. Don't we have enough money to build a small house? We got over $10,000."

"Yo Mama ain' had no bidness lettin' you know nothing 'bout how much we got. You ain' got no sense. Won' have a pot to piss in, listen to you."

"I tole the child how much we got and put her name on the bank book 'case somthin' happen to us. Somebody need to know. You don' never take 'sponsibility for nothin'. Always criticizin' me. You won' do mothin'."

"What you mean, I don' do nothin'. I work hard and bring the money home to you. You 'n this child wan' to run through all we got."

"Mama, why don' we see how much it would cost to build a little house?"

"You stop worryin' us to death! Every time I turn aroun' you worryin' me 'bout a house. Why don' you go do some work Clean up the house you got."

"Don't do no good to clean it up. Still looks a mess." I shouted. "Ya'll ain' go never do nothing. Make me sick. I'm sick of this shack we live in. Yal're all crazy."

"Who you callin' crazy? Yo Mama ain' raisin' you right. I'm-ma get my strop 'ware you out."

Papa started unbuckling his belt or heading for the razor strap that hung on a nail in the kitchen. If he ever got his belt off, I would take off running toward the woods, Papa shouting, "Gal, don't you run from me. I'm go kill you, y'hear."

Our discussion about renovating the house or building a new one usually ended in an impasse, either with me shouting and angry and in tears or with Papa threatening to kill me. Sometimes they would just clam up and refuse to talk about it. Then they made a revelation that both gave me a glimmer of hope, but shattered my immediate dreams.

I had cornered them together again.

"When we go fix up this place?"

"When you go leave us alone?"

"But Papa, we've been talkin' and talkin' about it and ya'll never <u>do</u> anything."

"Yeah, well cain't be puttin' money into this place 'n buildin' houses. This lan ain' our-en yet."

"What do you mean? Grandma owned this land."

"Yeah, but your Gran-ma died 'n she never left no will, so this lan ain' our-en."

"Mama, how come it's not ours?"

"Wa'll, Mama never left no will. I went to the lawyer. He say this lan won become mine till after seven years."

"<u>Seven years</u>?"

"Wal'll, yo Granma been dead a year, so we got six mo years and then maybe I kin get a deed. This heah is heirs property. Yo granma's second husband lef this lan, but Mama didn't leave no will. She coulda willed it me. Wouldna been no trouble."

"You mean we've got to wait six more years before we can build a house?"

Les don' be talkin' 'bout no house. If we git this lan---'n this a big if cause the heirs could contest it. But if we git this lan, we may kin sell som 'a it 'n get nuff money to maybe bil some kinna house."

"But we've already got $10,000. Why can't we just buy some more land and not wait <u>six whole years</u>."

"Stop talking 'bout money in heah. You want somebody to come in heah 'n kill us? Don' be hurrying nobody. I don tole yuh what I don tole yuh. Ef you jest let the good Lord work his way, we'll see what hap'ns."

"In six more years, I'll be in college. I'll be almost grown!"

"Thas another reason we cain' be spendin' all the money. You need to git a education so you won' hafta be 'pendin' on men. You worry 'bout gittin' you head fixed. We worry 'bout the house."

I was buoyed by that that <u>someday</u> (maybe) we would have a decent house. But six years meant that I would be ashamed to invite any friends all through high school. What a sad state of affairs.

****

At the end of seventh grade the school offered student with A or B averages an opportunity to attend summer school and skip to ninth grade. We would study eighth grade at an accelerated pace during the summer.

Lena and I chose to go to summer school, along with about fifteen or twenty other students. We studied English, math, science and American history. In the fall we entered ninth grade. We left the other students, some of whom we had known since elementary school, behind in eighth grade and joined an older group. For the rest of high school, I felt somewhat displaced.

Ninth grade moved by swiftly and at the end of the year, we graduated from junior high school. I was one of the top three in the class, along with another girl and boy.

For ninth grade graduation, Mama let me buy my first pair of nylon stockings. My hair was done for the occasion, and I had a crisp white voile dress. As one of the top three, I had to deliver a long oration about conservation. It sounded like something that had come from an exercise book for special occasions. The speech was six handwritten pages long. I had been memorizing it for over a month. Lena had threatened to try to make me mess up and forget my lines, so I was apprehensive about giving the speech.

The evening of graduation I dressed carefully. The new nylons felt a little baggy on my thin legs, but they also felt grown up. My hair hung over my shoulders and had had time for the grease to dissipate, so my hair looked naturally straight, full and buoyant. I admired myself in the mirror as the white neighbor girl, Jenny, watched me being transformed. She looked me carefully up and down. In admiration she turned her blue eyes on me and said, "My goodness, Oree, you look just like a nigger angel." I was both flattered and deflated.

The events went smoothly. I got through the speech without stumbling and Mama who was in the audience was proud of me, though she offered no compliments. Later I would hear her tell Papa, "That chile is real smart."

School

By the time I was in ninth grade I had begun to make friends. Lena and I had been friends since seventh grade, and continued our friendship throughout high school. In ninth grade we met Barbara, a short deep-brown skinned voluptuous girl with a slight stutter. Lena stuttered too, usually when she was excited.

We had begun to look at and talk about boys, Lena leading the way. By senior year all had lost their virginity except for me. Joyce had also joined our group, and two other girls occasionally ran with us.

We sat on the school grounds for lunch, swigging orange and grape sodas we bought from President's store, a tiny one-man operation that sold soft drinks and a variety of packaged snacks to the students at the school. To complete our meal, we ate small brown bags of parched peanuts we bought from an old man who sold them from a shed out of a burlap bag.

"Girl, did you see that new boy?"

"You mean the Spanish-looking boy with the bow legs?"

"Yeah. He is some kinda fine."

"He got a brother too."

"Sho nuff?"

"He's got lighter skin. He ain' as good lookin' as the other one, but he'll do."

"I found out his name is Allan---Allan Valencia---his brother name Raymond."

We spent the days following Allan and Raymond Valencia around the campus, giggling and trying to position ourselves so that we were in close proximity, especially to Allan.

Lena had begun to talk to a boy named Virgil Brown. His friend, Horace tried to talk to me. The whole process made me slightly uncomfortable. Finally, we made dates. Lena and I were to meet Virgil and Horace. Certainly, I did not want him to come to our house. So, a few days before Easter I told Mama that I was going to a movie with Lena on Easter. Mama and Papa had their own attitudes toward moviegoing on Sundays.

"You ain' got no bidness doing to the sho on a Sunday. Oughta be in church. The Lawd don' lak no foolishness on His day."

"Mama, ya'll're so old fashioned. What difference does it make?"

"All this goin' to the sho ain' no good."

"Well, can I go?"

"Ef you go to church first. We go to church, then we see. I don' lak it; Yo Papa go get mad."

I went to church with Mama. The sisters were sporting new hats and clothes, switching up and down the aisles to the collection plate, showing off their outfits. After church I caught the bus and went to the movie. Lena and I met Virgil and Horace. I was apprehensive. Lena had tried to school me many times in the fine art of kissing boys.

"You got to do French kissing."

I tried to act as though I knew all about French kissing. I had read about it in books, but had no practical experience.

"You know, you stick yo tongues in each other's mouth and suck."

Lena and I wore our Easter outfits. They were both light blue, of some form of newly processed pique. We both had pink, softly fuzzy short jackets. We had planned our similar outfits, putting them on Lay-a-way at Lerner's and paying a dollar a week.

We met the boys; they bought our 31 cent tickets, and walked up the four flights of stairs to the balcony of the Saenger Theater. I grew more and more nervous, knowing that the boys expected us to sit in the darkened theater and neck.

We found seats and sat down. Soon Horace turned my face to his and placed his lips next to mine. I figured now was the time to stick my tongue in his mouth. We sat there for two hours, Horace sucking on my tongue. I was not in the least affected by his slavering and sucking and was glad when the whole ordeal was over. My tongue was sore for a week.

I made up excuses not to join the three on similar "dates." Soon, Horace found a new girlfriend and I saw them from time to time walking about the campus or holding hands,

Horace walking her home. I was a bit jealous, but relieved.

Lena had also, much earlier told me how to do "it." She had spent the night with me and we had slept in the bed that Doris had slept in before she went to New York. Mama didn't especially like Lena, saying that she was "fast." Nevertheless, she agreed that Lena could spend the night. When the lights were out, we giggled until Mama yelled from the other room, "Stop that grinnin 'n go to sleep."

Lena said, "You know how to do it?" I had some notion from the many books I had read.

"Well," she said, "He puts his thing in you. Then you go up and down like this," she said, crawling on top of me.

I couldn't see what the big deal was supposed to be. I was glad when Lena stopped trying to show me by going up and down and got off.

Later, I began to worry about my femininity. I knew you were supposed to feel something, and I worried that Horace had failed to stir any excitement when he was sucking on my tongue at the Saenger.

I read a book about lesbians and began to worry that maybe I was a lesbian. Maybe Lena was a lesbian too. But Lena was all obsessed with boys. I was probably a lesbian, I thought. I examined my parts, wondering if all girls were made like me. Lena's talk didn't help.

"When you go do it?" Lena and Virgil had finally done it one night after a football game. He had bought rubbers and they had gone all the way. She was worried for a while that she might be pregnant, but finally her period came.

"They mus' be sum'pn wrong wit you," Lena said. "Don't you ever want to do it? Maybe you funny."

I became more anxious about my virginal state. I had no desire to do it. Mama had put the fear of God and men in me. I was terrified of getting pregnant. Mama said, "You keep yo dress down and yo drawers up. Dese ole boys git you in trouble. I cain be raisin' no mo babies. I'm too ole."

"You had your cou'ses yet? You messin wit dese boys? You be sorry."

I didn't like babies and knew I would not know what to do with one if Mama refused to take care of it. I wanted to do something with my life. I had begun to have negative feelings toward the whole institution of marriage and baby raising. I began to voice my opinions to Mama when she would broach the subject of getting a baby.

"You better stay 'way fom these ole boys, y'hear."

"I ain' studden these boys, Mama."

"Wa'll you wait til you git married."

"I'm not go ever get married."

"Wa'll I wouldn' say that."

"It's the truth. I'm not marryin' and I'm not havin' any babies. Look what marryin' and havin' babies got you. You 'n Papa don' even talk most of the time. All you get is washing the clothes, scrubbin' the floor, ironing, and workin' yourself to death. I'm going to have me a job. I don' want none of that drudgery."

"Wa'll we see."

I thought about Mama and Papa. I wondered if they ever did "it." They must have a long time ago, I thought, or else they couldn't have had four children. I couldn't see them still doing it, though. Mama slept in the bed with me. Papa slept in the little bed next to me. Maybe they got up in the middle of the night and did "it" while I was asleep. I couldn't believe that. No. Mama and Papa did not do "it."

Barbara finally hooked Allan Valencia. They did it. Barbara worried about being pregnant. I made up my mind that I would not do "it." "It" caused nothing but worry and heartache.

Lena had crushes. We all had crushes on Mr. Carter while in his tenth grade history class. Mr. Carter had wavy black straight hair---so called "good" hair. One day we were sitting in Mr. Carter's class. Mr. Carter had not entered the room. We were sitting two to a desk, talking, laughing, and cutting up. Lena came into the room; she reached my desk. Barbara turned around.

"Cccchile," Lena said.

"Cccchile," she repeated, trying to get out whatever she was trying to tell us.

"Mmmmmister Carter. Mmmmmmister Carter. Mmmmmmister Carter. He kissed me."

Lena started to laugh in her hysterical fashion. Barbara and I laughed uncontrollably,

Barbara gasping and my shoulders convulsed with the import of what Lena had just reported.

Mr. Carter came into the room. We looked at Mr. Carter and broke into uncontrollable laughter again, Lena going down on her knees in the aisle.

Mr. Carter finally managed to settle the class down, but all during class we cast sidelong glances at him and doubled up with laughter as we tried to outline Chapter 14 of our history books.

Lena had a crush on Mr. Baker. Mr. Baker, other than talking to her earnestly about civics, did not respond to her eye rolling and hip swinging. Lena found out he was engaged to a youngish teacher on the staff. She pined and cried even over Mr. Baker. Once I went into his room while he was out at an assembly and the room was empty. Lena was in the room walking around on the desk tops. I cried out in amazement, "Girl, are you crazy?"

Other boys sometimes tried to talk me into doing "it."

"Whut you savin' it for," they asked.

"Nature going to yo head. You gon go crazy."

I turned a deaf ear. I was not about to do "it."

School Continues

After seventh grade and the adjustments to large school life that it entailed, Lena and I settled into life in ninth grade as new members of the Class of '52.

School life consisted of trying to acquire an education in a school burgeoning beyond its capacity with young black children from the far reaches of the county. Often our classes were crowded. In seventh grade, traffic jams in the hallways resulted from too many students crammed into the single two-story building.

One afternoon when the bell rang, I was caught in a tremendous crush of young bodies on the upper floor. We were in the hallway that connected the two wings of the building. Bodies were jammed so tightly that my feet left the floor, and the old and fragile textbooks I tried to hold onto slipped from my hands. When the halls finally cleared, my social studies book had been trampled to shreds. Not a single page held to the tattered cover. I was without a book for the remainder of the year.

Movies were held in the mornings and afternoons to raise money for supplies. If we could muster the 25 cents charge, we were dismissed from classes to view the film in the auditorium. The school had bought black-out curtains, but somehow the images on the screen were barely discernable; nevertheless, we sat in the auditorium trying to make sense of the dim shadows that moved about on the screen. Given a choice between class and a movie, most students chose the latter, including me.

Ninth and tenth grade were hardly an improvement, and it was during tenth and eleventh grade that we began the habit of skipping English class, leaving the campus entirely and going to real movies at the Saenger Theater in the afternoons.

We had Miss Laverne Williams for English. She was a shy, silent woman, who it was rumored, had been jilted at the alter and who at no time taught anything. When we entered the room, six panels of the board were filled with sentences that we were to do one thing or the other with.

We would enter the room, take out our notebooks, and proceed to perform the designated operations on the sentences. Miss Williams sat at her desk smiling. A few brown nosers would go up to the desk and talk to Miss Williams, admire her hair which she arranged always in the same ancient style, rolls of curls held by bobby pins covering the front of her head, and the rest of her hair pulled into a large roll at the back. Some of the girls would try to comb Miss Williams's long hair, and several actually succeeded in cajoling her into letting them take her hair down.

We studied no literature. The sole lesson in lit was an assignment to read Sarah Kimbell Knight's description of a journey she once took.

The students talked incessantly during these class periods, occasionally throwing spitballs, and engaging in various nonsense to break the monotony, growing louder and louder as the period progressed.

At some point during the year, Lena and I hit on the idea of skipping this travesty altogether and going to the movie. It was our last class, so we simply never reported, instead, sneaking around the front of the building, heading a block down Cervantes, and then walking down A Street to Gregory and on to the Saenger.

Many of our afternoons were spent in the darkened balcony of the Saenger. Occasionally, Barbara joined us. The movie that made the greatest impression on us was "Knock on any Door" with John Derek. We promptly all fell in love with Derek, admiring his full shock of dark wavy hair. We spent endless hours discussing him, the movie, and even affected a gesture that he had used in the film whenever we parted.

One afternoon, we had just turned onto A Street and were heading toward Gregory. We were thrown into confusion when we glanced up and heading toward us in his late model car was the principal, Dr. G. T. Wiggins. He glanced at us just as he passed, smiled and waved.

We had had no time to devise a strategy. We could not run, so we waved back and decided to continue our hike. For a few days we expected to be called to the office and maybe even suspended, but nothing ever happened. Perhaps Dr. Wiggins thought we had legitimate business on the streets at 1:45 in the afternoon, or maybe he had too many other things to think of. We continued our moviegoing throughout eleventh grade, having drawn Miss Williams for English again.

When we were seniors, we went to English class, having acquired a more alert and lively teacher; however, we slipped into the habit of skipping phys ed. I despised phys ed, having skinny legs that I despaired of revealing in the white short one-piece uniform we wore to dress out. We went to a couple of classes and learned the theory of the games of volleyball and basketball; then when it was time to dress out, we simply stopped going. We wandered around campus when we were supposed to be in class and often left the campus to go to a store on Reus Street. Once we were almost apprehended coming from the store eating the sweets we had bought. We skipped all through first semester. Then, in second semester, we acquired an intern from Florida A & M University. Apparently, she checked roll. After several weeks, she reported us to the assistant principal, Mr. Wallace.

We were hauled into the office. I was terrified. What would Mama and Papa say and do? Probably kill me.

We stood before Mr. Wallace.

"It's been reported that you girls have missed physical education for an extended period of time. The procedure for such infractions of the rules is suspension." Lena looked at me. I looked at the floor.

"What do you girls have to say for yourselves?"

We couldn't think of anything to say. Suddenly, Mrs. Alice Lovely, who had been my shorthand teacher for a brief while, came in.

"Orastine, what you doin' in here?"

"They've been skippin' class."

"Nooo, not these girls. They're nice girls," addressing us, "You ever been in any trouble before?"

"No," we said hastily, speaking up for the first time. "Please, Mrs. Lovely, tell Mr. Wallace not to suspend us," we pleaded.

Mrs. Lovely said, "I know this child's family. She's a good girl. She won't do it again, will you?" she said, looking at me. Mrs. Lovely was a somewhat impish kind of woman who seemed to secretly enjoy to a certain extent our flaunting of the rules.

Mr. Wallace relented. "All right," he said, "if you stay in class for the rest of the year." We agreed.

I had had Mr. Wallace for a while for chemistry. He spent little time teaching chemistry and devoted most of his energies to being a combination dean and assistant principal. After he let us off, we would go by and talk with him, Lena hoping to get a glance at Mr. Carter, who also sometimes hung out in Mr. Wallace's office. Sometimes if I needed to type out an announcement, I would use the battered typewriter in his office, the one that he used to peck out memos with two fingers.

One day Lena and I were in the office. He said, "You girls want to go out?" I couldn't believe Mr. Wallace was propositioning us. I knew he couldn't come to my house, and I did not relish him as a date. He was old and bald headed and married. He indicated that Mr. Carter wanted to take Lena out, and he would like to spend some time with me. I tried to think of a response that wouldn't get myself into his bad graces. After all, he had let us off without punishment. I didn't know whether Lena would go so far as to go out with Mr. Carter. I don't think any of us really thought beyond flirting with the men, though I figured Lena would be more apt to accept than I.

"Where you live," he asked me.

"Out Davis," I said, being vague.

"Where on Davis," he persisted.

"Well, not exactly on Davis, but off Davis."

I never did tell Mr. Wallace exactly where. He made some plans that involved Mr. Carter and Lena and him and me. I was flabbergasted. What would Mama think? Surely, Mr. Wallace didn't expect to come driving up to my house. I felt a little in collusion with the clandestine plans, and wondered whether I had somehow given Mr. Wallace the idea that I would agree. Lena was pretty obvious in her desire for something, and I guessed that Mr. Wallace thought that since I was Lena's friend, I was out for the same thing.

I stayed out of Mr. Wallace's office for a long time. Evidently he forgot about the plans. At least he did not mention them again.

Most of the lessons I learned in school either did not concern the lessons taught in class or were learned through my own efforts rather than the efforts of my teachers. There were some excellent teachers---Mrs. Jones, the algebra and geometry teachers, was soft spoken, but explained the algebra so that it was child's play to me. When the class grew loud, she would stand there and speak in a very low voice; finally we calmed down to hear what she said. She addressed us all as "Miss Dawson," "Miss Jenkins," or "Mr. Brown." She said we were old enough for some respect.

Mr. Andrews, the biology teacher in tenth grade, drew clear models and was thorough. We trusted Mr. Andrews and he was kind and funny. He lent us money that we never repaid and always called me "Grandma" because I was so slow and backward socially. He called me Grandma until I was a young woman teaching at the school.

Some of the teachers devised interesting and challenging units that involved students. Our seventh grade social studies teachers concocted a unit study of South American culture and ended our study with a gigantic fiesta that kicked off with a program in the auditorium and went on all day with us in our South American costumes.

One of our home economics teachers in eleventh grade had us report to her house after school where we baked the most delicious cookies from her personal collection of recipes. We baked cookies until late in the evening. We had already planned a tea for the kindergarten children whose school was on A Street. We took the cookies and punch and entertained the children with games.

The evening we baked the cookies, we had stayed past dark. Mrs. Goode insisted on taking Lena and me home. I was mortified. I did not want her to see where I lived. But she would not relent.

As we drew closer to my house, I flushed and was silent. She insisted on coming in and talking to Mama whose older children she had taught when she was a younger teacher.

The next day she said, "Your grandmother has done what she could to make an attractive home. You must learn all you can so that you can do even better when you get your own home." Somehow, she had found something positive to say. I silently thanked her.

In twelfth grade English, six weeks before school ended we were given a major assignment. We were to read some twenty novels and write detailed reports of them, and also write an original play. I had always done my assignments religiously, but this seemed overwhelming. True, I read all the time, but twenty novels in six weeks?

Blacks did not use the county's public library, and our school library did not contain many of the books. I went to the public library and asked to check out the other books. The librarian eyed me suspiciously. I explained that I was a student at Washington High School; I told her about the assignment and the time limit. She looked at me. "Do you have a library card?"

I said I did not. The Woman must have seen my desperation, for she took my list and went into the stacks and returned with battered copies of the books I needed. I took the books home. <u>The Last of the Mohicans.</u> I read enough to get the drift of the story. <u>Moby Dick</u>, <u>The House of Seven Gables</u>, <u>The Scarlet Letter</u>, <u>Huckleberry Finn</u>, <u>Emerson's Essays</u>, <u>Pride and Prejudice</u>. I knew and recognized the titles. Knew these were books I should have read and vowed someday to do so. I read <u>Huck Finn</u> and "Self-Reliance," finding a life-long credo.

I did my best to understand the gist of the books, but ended up fudging on the complete reading. In writing my reports, I started with the parts I had read, somehow reaching what I thought were the right conclusions.

I typed my report on an ancient typewriter that my neighbors had let me borrow. When I received my report back, I had received an A++. I doubted that Mrs. Harris had read any of it. Mrs. Harris was notorious for dragging students out of the commencement line for failure to turn in THE REPORT. Students struggled to finish their work. How they did it without books, I never knew. Most managed to pass.

Manhattan

The summer after tenth grade Mama and I went to New York. I was fourteen. The year was 1950. Mr. Garrison, our neighbor, drove us to the L and N Station in his ancient Ford. We carried a box lunch of fried chicken, ham, light bread, and thick slices of pound cake. This lunch would have to sustain us over the long trip since blacks could not eat in the dining car and Mama would have balked at paying the prices even if we could have.

It was around eight o'clock in the evening as the train pulled out. We stopped in Flomaton and changed to the Hummingbird, a fast train that had become legendary in my mind through Doris's descriptions of it on her annual trips home.

When day dawned, we were pulling into the small Georgia town of West Point. We sat in the car reserved for blacks. The train began its long climb up from the Southland---through Atlanta and Richmond. As the train pulled into Washington D.C., my pulses began to quicken. Soon we would be in the North, the fabled home of damn Yankees. I strained to see more of the nation's capital, but was confined to looking at railroad tracks and the shabby parts of town that bordered them.

Near Wilmington, Delaware, I was aware of a haziness that seemed to dim the sun. Giant smokestacks belched puffs of black smoke that scattered out over the city. On to Philadelphia, then Trenton, New Jersey, and at last Pennsylvania Station, New York City.

I wore a blue and white rayon, geometrically printed dress and ill-fitting white shoes. It was probably late June. Mama and I gathered together our hand-luggage, tied with string that Papa insisted on tying around it, and stood in the aisle, waiting to detrain.

Once we stepped off the train, we followed the other passengers through a maze of passageways and up an escalator, into the main waiting room. It was huge. The vastness of things took my breath away. A group of young black men, standing by a newsstand, leered at me, eager to pounce on fresh country meat. Seeing Mama, they turned their gaze to the other passengers streaming up from the train. We stood in confusion, peering at the faces in the crowd, trying to spy Doris, Silas, and Mary. Suddenly Doris materialized and instantaneously was hugging and kissing Mama and me. Then Uncle Silas's mustache tickled my face, and I greeted Mary shyly.

We were hustled out of the station. Outside, the height of the buildings astounded me. I had little time to gape as Doris and Silas shoved us into a cab. The sun was shining, but appeared weak and its light diluted. I stared out the window of the cab at the incredible height of the buildings, trying to answer Doris's questions and absorb the full import of my surroundings. The cab lurched through traffic---more traffic than I had ever seen---at an incredible speed. I unconsciously braked with the cabbie, fully expecting to crash into oncoming vehicles that appeared out of nowhere and veered off at crazy angles.

We stayed in New York for two weeks. Most of our time was spent on Lymon Place in the Bronx where Doris lived. It was different living upstairs and looking out over the city. The apartment was neatly kept, but Doris waged a losing battle trying to keep the city's black, sooty dust off the floor of her apartment. Going barefoot as I was accustomed to, my soles were caked with a thick crust of greasy, black dirt.

We went on excursions to the fabled tourist attractions I had seen in the movies or heard of on the radio---the Empire State Building, the Bronx Zoo, Times Square. We browsed in Macy's and Gimble's. I bought a pair of gray suede loafers in Gimbel's shoe department, Mama complaining about the price. I saw the famed Rockettes at Radio City Music Hall. The size of the place left me feeling dwarfed. Our Saenger Theater could not compare. Jerry Lewis and Dean Martin performed. Mama and I traveled by subway to Harlem, the home of the Apollo Theater and birth place of the Harlem Renaissance. The sidewalk vegetable stands fascinated me, and Fred who lived in Harlem with Connie, Laverne, and Phillip, took me for walks about the teeming streets, filled with brown and black men and women hurrying to their appointed destinations. Fred took us on the long subway ride to Coney Island. I strolled on the boardwalk, and Fred and I rode the Tornado, a giant rollercoaster. I felt my body leave my stomach at the top of the mountain as we plunged down. When the ride was up, we promptly bought another ticket. Mama said, "You fool; you go git yoself kilt."

In New York I first encountered the multiracial dimension of the American populace. In Pensacola everyone was either black or white. Here, Indians from the Far East, Puerto Ricans, European immigrants---Italians, Irishmen, Jews---all mingled in a crazy-quilt of diversity. I had never heard a language other than English spoken except in the movies, and the mingled tongues of these varied men and women jangled in my ears. People in native dress drew my stares. Mary and I went to movies in Bronx neighborhood theaters on Southern Boulevard. Spanish-speaking immigrants were beginning to inhabit the Bronx, and the polyglot strollers were infinitely fascinating.

We had left Papa behind in Pensacola, and he and his brother Colbert, who had come to spend the two weeks with him, were left to fend for themselves. Papa must have been overcome with loneliness for although he could not write, he managed to scribble out a few lines and mail them to us in New York.

I had never been separated from Papa, and suddenly I was seized with a strange dread that he would die while we were away and I would never see him alive again. When I was not being overwhelmed by the immensity of New York, I worried for Papa's safety back in Pensacola.

We left New York and returned to Pensacola on the Silver Comet, another fast train. In Atlanta, my period started. I whispered the fact to Mama. I could think of nothing to do and feared I would be a bloody mess by the time the train arrived in Pensacola the next day, but Mama questioned an attendant; then she said, "You stay heah and watch our things. I'll be back."

I was nervous without Mama by my side. Suppose we missed the train. Suppose she got lost and was gobbled up by Atlanta, no small town itself. Suppose. Suppose.

Mama came back promptly with Kotex in a brown paper bag. She had walked down the street somewhere to a store. I was impressed with Mama's courage.

When we exited the train at Flomaton, I blinked as the dazzlingly bright sunlight struck my eyes. After two weeks, I had grown accustomed to the muted light of the industrialized Northeast. I could not imagine people who spent their entire lives in that vast city, always deprived of the vivid skies of my native Florida.

Senior year, the teachers at Washington High School ruled that the homecoming queen had to have at least a B+ average to compete in the election to be chosen Miss WHS. I had never dreamed of being chosen homecoming queen, for I knew that my peers did not consider me that type.

I was viewed as something of an eccentric genius who consistently received good grades, but definitely not a part of the social scene. I had gone to only one football game, accompanied by Papa who refused to let me travel to the west side of town alone at night. Papa had finally agreed to take me to a game after a stormy scene prior to the game before.

"Why can't I go to the game?"

"You cain't be runnin' round in these streets at night. Somebody knock you in the head."

"But everybody goes to the games. I'm the only person who never goes. I've never even been to a game."

"You ain' everybody 'n you ain' miss nothing. You cain go."

"But why? I could go on the bus and transfer to another bus."

"I say you cain go, and you cain go.'"

"I don't never get to go nowhere."

"You don' need to be runnin' roun at night by yoself."

"I'm going anyway!"

"You won' leave outta this house tonight!"

"I will."

"You do, I beat yo butt!"

"I don't care."

"Don' be sayin' you don' care."

"I don't; I'm going!"

"You go, you git a killin. Thas all I got to say. I don' wan to heah no mo about it!"

I gave up, bursting into tears. But the next time I asked, Papa said he would take me to the game. This was definitely not what I had bargained for. I was embarrassed, but I went to the game. Papa stood around on a hill apart from the crown and paced about until the game was over. Only a few classmates found out he was my grandfather.

When the girls eligible for homecoming queen and court were announced, my name was among them, since I had one of the highest averages in the class, and the beautiful people had been eliminated because of their grades. I knew that I would not be queen, for a well-rounded popular athletic girl who played basketball was also among the group, but I longed to be a member of the court.

The election was held, and the basketball player was chosen queen. I was number three. I was thrilled.

We were told that we needed an evening dress for a photograph the next day. Mama said, "I cain' get no evening dress for tomorrow. I'm going to buy you one for the parade, but I ain' got no way to git no dress for tomorrow."

"What about my hair?" I asked, despairing of the two braids I wore wound into balls on the sides of my head.

"You jus have to do the best you kin wit it. You kin go to the hairdresser for the parade. These teachers don' give nobody time fur nothin'."

I borrowed a dress from Wilma Jean Powell, one of the neighborhood whites for the photo. It was an old unstylish bluish satin gown, not very appealing. I had bought a straightening comb, and I tried to straighten my own hair. The picture turned out not too bad, but far from what I had dreamed. My hair looked bushy, almost like later afro styles. The other girls must have had the same problem with dresses, for theirs didn't look much better than mine.

The day of the parade I dressed in the new gown Mama had bought. It was a tangerine-colored dress with thin straps, a taffeta underskirt, and layers of tangerine netting and ruffles as was the fashion of the times. My hair cascaded to my shoulders, and I applied makeup that I had begun to wear in tenth grade. I admired my final transformation from ugly duckling to radiant swan.

Mama and Papa had agreed to let me spend the night of the parade and game with Barbara who lived on the West side. Barbara was not a member of the court, but I would ride the float and get off at Mrs. Jones's house where the parade disbanded and walk to Barbara's house and dress and go with her to the game.

Riding the float, I smiled and drew stares from admiring onlookers. With the gorgeous people eliminated and in the first full revelation of my flowering, I was the prettiest girl on the float.

In a euphoric state when we reached Mrs. Jones's house and were helped down from the float, I was eager to get to Barbara's for the rest of the night. Barbara's house was a long walk from Mrs. Jones's on Reus Street to West Wright Street.

I set out, wearing my tangerine gown, walking as briskly as I could manage in high-heeled shoes to Cervantes Street. It had grown dark, and the streets were poorly lighted. Headlights of cars caught me in their revealing glare. I kept walking down "A" Street. As I approached Jackson Street, a car cruising slowly to the corner caught my eye. As the car slowly passed me, I saw the mask-like face of a young white man staring from the driver's seat. My heartbeat quickened. I walked a bit faster, trying to calm my racing thoughts. As I neared the next corner, the car appeared again. I was sure this time that the driver had evil intent. The car cruised slowly past. I turned the corner. I was only about three blacks from Barbara's house. Glancing over my shoulder, I saw the car approaching slowly from behind. I moved instinctively to the far side of the pavement. The car cruised slowly until it was even with me. The man said, "Hey! Git in."

I accelerated into a run, going as fast as my long gown and high-heeled shoes permitted. I turned the last corner before Barbara's house, running now at full speed, holding my dress up with one hand, occasionally tripping in the high heels. The car had slowed again. I dashed onto Barbara's porch, banging on the door. In a swift side-long glance, I saw the car turn the corner and accelerate speed.

Barbara opened the door. Panting, I stumbled into the living room.

"What's the matter wit you, girl? You look like you seen a gos!"

I thought, Jesus, Papa was right.

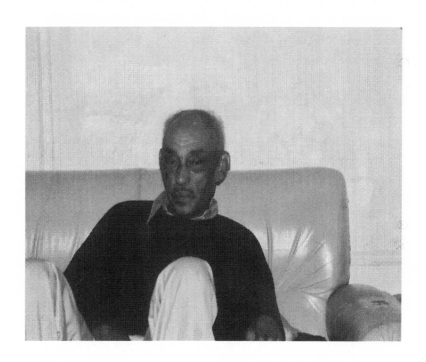

Burn

We lived way out in the country, and people thought nothing of hauling their trash to the nearest clearing or alongside a road and dumping it out of their cars. They let their livestock and dogs wander about at will, and they burned trash and set fire to the woods when they pleased.

Mama and Papa and Grandma too, just before spring, would set the fields around our house on fire. I suppose these were efforts at controlled burning. They said the fires eradicated insects and plant diseases. These burnings were always a source of excitement for me, and after the fields were scorched black, I would scavenge the areas, often finding pecans dropped by birds that had snatched them off pecan trees all over Brent in the fall. When I spied a nut, I would pick it up and crack it open with my teeth and eat the meat which had a roasted, smoky taste that I relished.

If there were laws against setting these fires, we were blissfully ignorant of them. The environmentalists hadn't got going then, and we were governed only by our own sense of propriety. Perhaps we did no harm since the only house that we conceivably might have burned would have been our own. This was always a danger since our house was already a fire trap without the additional hazard of flying sparks from a brush fire. Indeed, in the dead of winter, when Papa got a fire roaring in both fireplaces, sparks would sometimes shoot up the chimney, and we would all go outside in the cold and stare nervously at the roof to see if any of them had ignited the rotten, powdery shingles that covered the house.

One time when Uncle Silas, my Aunt Doris's husband, had accompanied her down from New York for a winter visit, he was determined that it was past time for a bath, being a city slicker who was accustomed to showering every morning and night. But he was reluctant to strip down in front of the fireplace because he had found out that your backside always froze while your front-side was scorched and your legs were spotted from continuous sitting in front of the fire in winter. That night, Papa put the tub in front of the fireplace and filled it with water. Then he commenced to pile wood on the fire so Uncle Silas could keep warm while maintaining proper personal hygiene. Pretty soon sparks were shooting up the chimney and flying over the roof like winter lightning bugs and threatening to burn us out of house and home. The soot inside the chimney had ignited, and we were all outside watching the sparks jumping out the chimney. Uncle Silas's bathwater cooled down, and he never did get his bath. From then on, he and Doris came to Florida in the summer.

Anyway, usually when the adults set the ten acres on fire, they would be prepared with brush brooms to beat out the fire if it threatened to come too close to the house.

Sometimes, though, I would become impatient, thinking that the older ones would never get around to starting the fires, and I would take matches and go down in the woods behind the house and start a few myself. The first couple of times, as the fire burned a small area, I grew anxious and stamped it out.

The last time I started such a blaze, I had been waiting with anticipation for the adults to initiate the ritual, but they were either too busy with more pressing concerns or had simply decided that the woods could do without a burning that year.

Unable or unwilling to wait longer, I got together a handful of matches and went down into the woods below the house.

I found a chip of brick, struck the match, and watched as the dry brown grass ignited, shriveled up and lit other blades. The fire was soon crackling and burning in an ever-widening circle.

As the fire ate its way along, it crept closer and closer to the taller grasses and straw at the edge of what had been the fenced portion of our land.

Suddenly, a breeze kicked up, sweeping the blaze rapidly toward our top two acres. I tried to stomp out the blaze, but its circumference had widened so that by the time I pounded on one part of the semi-circle, the blaze at the opposite end, with the help of the breeze, had reignited and was mowing down the dry brown grass and straw that covered the outer edges of our top two acres.

I ran home screaming, ripping my legs through nascent blackberry vines.

"Somebody set the woods on fire! Somebody set the woods on fire! It's coming this way!" I hollered.

By the time the grownups got together the brooms and other fire-fighting materials, the blaze had reached the tall straw that grew near the house.

Mama and Grandma and I tried to beat out the blaze, but it was raging too intensely. Sparks and flying ash from disintegrating leaves drifted down, settling in our hair. I imagined that was what snow would look like if it snowed in Florida. The fire had eaten its way into the taller trees that were now a blazing wall behind the smoking straw.

Mama and Grandma stared in dismay at the blaze.

"Lawdy, mercy," Mama said, "Might 's well let it burn out. Jes pray none a them sparks don set the ole shack on fire."

The fire raged on, trees snapping and popping and hissing. I could feel the blaze, hot against my face, as I stood mesmerized by the destruction I had set in motion. A secret wish floated in my head. If the old house burned down, surely we would replace it with a better one. But then I would hate to lose my comic books. Maybe I could get them out in time. I ran to the house and gathered together my Batman's and Wonder Woman's. You understand that I did not set out to burn down the house, but if it had happened, what a marvelous bit of serendipity.

We stood watching the progress of the fire, Mama and Grandma casting anxious glances toward the house. Miraculously, the blaze died down and stopped---right at the edge of the sandy yard by the clothes line. Heck, the old house was indestructible. It had survived all manner of hurricanes and hot sparks in all its awful ugliness.

"I wisht I knowed who set them woods on fire," Grandma said, hands on her hips and listening intently for signs of the arsonists.

"Probably some a them ole no good boys y'see layin' round heah," Mama scoffed.

I figured it was time for me to take a walk.

Soon the smoldering woods would cool off, and I would skip through them to find the scorched nuts, and later the grass would send tiny green shoots to carpet the ground; new leaves would grace the trees, and the yellow straw would wave again in the breeze. Maybe I'd get lucky and the next time the fire would take the old house away.

Mama

Mama said Grandma put her in the kitchen when she was nine years old, and she never got out. Understandable, since Grandma was a woman of action and affairs with little time for household chores. Mama stayed at home, cooked, cleaned, and did housework for whites who lived within walking distance.

Mama suffered from various ailments, and I can still see her with three or four of the wide leaves of jimson weed tied around her head to cure one of her frequent headaches.

Mama was not an affectionate person; she rarely distributed hugs and kisses. She demonstrated her love through the tasks she did for you. She was busy from before sunup until late at night. She was nosey, a busybody who always wanted to know the neighborhood gossip. If anybody's husband was unfaithful, anybody's daughter pregnant, anybody a drunkard or a gambler, Mama knew.

On the way to the store we would stop by the Wallaces or the McPhersons, or the Donalds. Later, I would hear her telling Doris or Grandma.

"Esther got rid a that baby. Been layin' outta school. Some rich boy's chile. Rekin he paid fuh it."

"They say X funny; you know, laks mens."

"Billy Bob, he beat Emma Jean. Beat dat 'oman all de time. Wouldn' stay wit no man beat me."

"Ole lady S, she so nasty. I saw her washin' dat young'un in de sink whare she washes dishes. Wouldn' eat nothin' she cook."

"You oughtta see dat ole greasy dress Ole Lady M had on. Dat Dressuz greasy fom her titties t' her knees. Some white foks sho is nasty."

I knew the neighbor's secrets. When I saw them, I wondered if it were all true. Certainly, Mama didn't lie. I figured everybody had a side they presented to the world and a hidden side that was only talked about in whispers.

Mama and Grandma fought all the time. Not hand to hand com bat, but they were endlessly sniping at each other. Grandma would start it:

"My dominecker pullet gone; thought I saw her ova in yo pen."

"That pullet mine; had it since it was a biddy."

"That my same dominecker pullet. You jes don conered it up in yo pen."

"You cuzin' me a stealin' yo pullet?"

"I ain' cuzin' nobody a nothin', jus sayin' the truth."

"What I wanna steal a chicken fuh?"

"My pullet gone."

"Maybe som'pn caught yo pullet."

"Ain' nothin' caught that pullet."

"How you know?"

"I know whare my pullet is."

"I get tied you 'cuzin' me takin' yo ole chickens. Oughtta be 'shamed 'a yo'self. You kin have the ole pullet, you want 'im. You wan' the pullet?"

"You ain' right, sister; you ain' right."

Grandma would stir up the devil, then lapse into song, singing or humming a hymn, ignoring Mama. Mama would be fit to be tied.

One evening about four o'clock Mama and I went to the store. We bought a watermelon and were bringing it home in a net sack, the kind oranges usually came in. We took the long way home so Mama could stop by Colleen's house on the way back. We left the watermelon outside by the side of the road.

We stayed in Colleen's for over an hour, Colleen and Mama sharing the neighborhood gossip, The talked and talked, Colleen having moved from closer to our house and behind in the gossip. When we left Colleen's, we didn't think about the watermelon.

About halfway down the road, we spied three or four children dragging our sack. Mama yelled, "Put that watermelon down. That's our watermelon."

The children ran off, but when we caught up with the sack, we found that the watermelon had been cracked open. Mama said, "Wa'll, jes leave it there. We gut us another watermelon sometime. Nasty stinkin' devils."

I was mad. Mama's love of gossip had cost me a juicy treat.

Grandma had a habit of bringing preachers home for Sunday dinner. Doris and Mama and later just Mama would have fixed a good dinner: two or three fried chicken, potato salad, macaroni and cheese, fresh vegetables, egg custard pies or banana pudding; then unexpectedly, Grandma and the preachers would show up.

Mama and Doris plotted to fix Grandma.

Sunday morning Grandma went off to church as usual, leaving Doris and mama to cook dinner. Doris and Mama set about cooking as usual. I could hear them giggling and plotting in the kitchen, but paid no special attention.

About two o'clock Grandma and the preachers drove up. I heard Grandma say, "Come on in; have some dinner."

One of the preachers said, "Don' min if we do."

Grandma and the preachers sat around talking church business for a while. "Dinner bout ready?" Grandma inquired.

"Few mo minits," Mama said.

Finally the preachers were shown into the kitchen.

Mama and Doris had fixed a surprised meal of black eyed peas and cornbread. *Grandma* was fit to be tied.

Waiting

I spent the summer when school was out
reading or going to the movies. I continued to read
the works in the old anthologies I found around
the house, the English romantic poets: Shelly,
Keats, Byron, especially appealed to me. I read
Milton and Wordsworth's poetry.

Still reading comic books, fan magazines,
romance stories, I drifted into Somerset Maugham,
reading Of Human Bondage and The Moon and
Sixpence. Later, I read Black Boy and Native Son,
and became fascinated with Greek and Roman
mythology. The Wonder Woman comic book had
led me into mythology. It was in mythology that I
read about the House of Atreus. I wondered if
some distant ancestor had brought a curse on our
family. Mama, Papa, and Grandma seemed
unlikely prospects. It must have been someone
long before. I wondered about my white
ancestors---could one of them be the guilty one?
Black and Indian ancestors were hazy entities that
I could not cause to materialize. Then, maybe the
family's bad luck was the testing of Job. "There
was a good man in the land of Uz"---I wondered if
Papa were being tested and how many more of us
would die.

Thinking about the Job story led me to
thinking about God. I had read enough science and
was so much a product of the scientific thought of

the age as to wonder if there even were a god.
None of it seemed to make sense. Mama certainly
talked about The Lawd enough, but Mama went to
church only infrequently. On Sunday evenings she
would sit propped up against a tree, reading the
Bible to Papa, but still did not seem especially
devout. Papa never went to church at all, though
he occasionally mentioned The Lawd.

I had read all of the Bible stories in a thick
Bible comic book and had read enough in the Bible
to question some of its logic. Sometimes I talked to
Papa.

"Papa," I said, "You know how in the Bible it
says that Adam and Eve had two sons---Cain and
Abel? Well, Cain killed Abel. Then the Bible says
Cain went somewhere and took a wife. Who did he
marry, Papa? The Bible says there were just the
four of them, and then Seth."

"Wa'll, you know, mens wrote the Bible."

"I know, but it's supposed to be the word of
God."

"Wa'll you never kin tell whut things mean
in the Bible. It don' mean whut it say, but it do.
You spose to b'leve it on faith."

I could not garner enough faith to believe it
all. I had not joined the church. I had never had a
"religious" experience. Too, I did not relish being
dipped in the cold water of the creek.

My surroundings, the natural world were
inspiring to me, both comforting and disturbing. I
spent endless nights gazing at the stars. I had read
what I could in the limited school science books---

knew the names of stars, planets, and constellations. The vastness of it all sobered me. What did it all mean? Where had it come from? Did someone or something create it or did it just come to be? Why did William and my mother die? Was there a reason, or did it just happen? If it just happened, what did that mean about what might happen to Mama and Papa and me? Why did things have to die anyway?

I was intrigued by cloud formations and the power of hurricanes. I ordered a book about clouds and learned the names of the various formations and identified them as they floated overhead.

Ants fascinated me. I watched them for hours. Sometimes digging up their mounds and watching them proceed to reconstruct their empire. The next day the mound would be more or less reconstructed.

I was interested in everything. I listened to broadcasts from the Met on Saturday evenings, learning the names of opera composers. Somewhere I picked up the names and accomplishments of artists, writers, architects.

I listened to the McCarthy hearings on the radio and followed the Korean War. I remember being accused of being a smart aleck because of a teacher's confusion. We were talking in class, being inattentive. The teacher said "Why don' ya'll shut up. You're so stupid you don' even know the war is over."

Having been following the Korean War with interest, I blurted out incredulously, "Is the war over?"

"Don' try to be funny," she said. "People oughtn't to be so stupid."

She had reference to the Second World War that had ended in 1945. Attuned to the present, I had reference to the "conflict" in Korea. All day I waited to get home to listen to the news. I thought I had somehow missed an important event. That night I found out the war was not over.

I lay awake in bed late into the night, listening to the sound of the midnight train. The long, lonesome blasts on the whistle filled me with restlessness. I wanted to be everywhere at once. Why had I been fated to this small Gulf Coast town? Reading novels, I had learned that artists and writers had gravitated to Paris for years. I wanted to join them. Maybe they could answer my questions. I would like to talk to Hemingway and Fitzgerald. (I did not know that Fitzgerald had already died.)

In my mind I could move back and forth in time; group odd assemblages of individuals. In my head I talked back and forth with illustrious people and wandered strange streets, familiar from descriptions in books.

I expected to go to college, but I longed for impossible schools---Harvard and Yale. But in the end I settled for the newly opened black junior college. I received a scholarship that paid tuition, and I continued to live with Mama and Papa in the same tumble-down house, still waiting out the long six years...and still dreaming.

Black Girl Dreaming

I grasped my spun-gold lasso and whirled out
a perfect loop, catching the fleeing interloper; the
rope tightened, holding him fast. Spinning about, I
deflected a hail of speeding bullets with my Amazon
wristband. His accomplice turned and fled as I leapt
in twenty-foot bounds, closing the space in a
fraction of a second, and landing a stunning blow to
his jaw, which caved inward on contact.

A vicious jolt brought me back out of the
reverie, and I became aware of the other bodies
packed into the bus as we bumped along, heading
out Davis Highway. I slipped the comic book I had
already finished into my notebook, reached up
and pulled the cord to signal the driver to stop.
The bus slowed, stopped; the back door opened,
and I stepped out and headed down the road.

"Baby, come on, chile. Put that thing down.
We got to hang out these clothes. Don't you ever
get tired, readin' all that mess? You go ruin yo
eyes. What you see in that foolishness, anyway?
Lawd have mercy. The chile gon go crazy. Do yo
school work."

"Already finished."

Papa sprawled on the edge of the front
porch, lying on his side in his dusty work clothes,
smoking his pipe. A thin white stream curled
upward, diffusing in the evening air. The scent of
burning tobacco mixed with the cloying smell of

honeysuckle sending tendrils out, snaking into the taller trees.

Chickens with wings drooping, beaks parted, in the hot heavy air. Lying in the hammock reading. Keats.

"A thing of beauty is a joy forever."

A jelly glass of cold lemonade on the ground. Grains of sand sticking to the moist bottom. Beads of sweat pearling on the sides.

Pitch black. Stars. The nebulous path of the Milky Way.

"You going to work for us. Be our maid."

"Naw. Studying business. Going to be a secretary."

"Who gon hire you?"

"Make a fine maid."

I tossed my dark, luxuriant hair back, ran my hands over its rippling waves, and thought about Nicky. The wedding was only a few days off. It was comforting to dream of our life together. It would be a continuation of all that I had been born to. Only with his love, I could escape some of the demands of my public life and the solicitous concerns of my family. Our honeymoon. The bright sun and sparkling waters of the Mediterranean, and after that...

It was night. Hot. My eyes flew open and I could see Papa's form sprawled out on the little bed next to the iron four-poster Mama and I slept in. Beyond Papa's bed I could see the open door and make out one of the crepe myrtles and the shadowy clumps of bushes that were Mama's

flower beds, now drained of color. The path
leading from the doorstep wound on toward the
rutted road which connected other unpaved roads
leading west. Sacred. Something, who knows what,
could come down the path while we lay
vulnerable. I pulled the cover over my head,
curled into a ball, and drowned in my own sweat.

Midday. I lay partially on the cool boards
and partially on the prickly oriental rug that
covered the floor in Grandma's room. Hot. I had
crawled under Grandma's bed and lay there
reading a tattered literature anthology that had
once belonged to one, or serially perhaps to all, of
my uncles and aunts or maybe to my dead mother.
Milton. "The mind is its own place, and in itself can
make a Heaven of Hell, a Hell of Heaven." It was
true. The preacher lied.

"Where you at, chile? Why you always layin'
round? Won't mount to a hilla beans. Lawd have
mercy. Go wash them dishes."

I stood staring down into the murky water
of the rain barrel standing near the corner of the
lean-to kitchen. Its contents had receded, and it
was only about one-fourth full. An iridescent film
covered the surface. I dropped a stick in and
watched wiggle tails corkscrew away with the
eddies. The water looked black and teemed with
infectious organisms.

I headed past the chicken pen, down the
path toward the outhouse. On either side, tangled
blackberry vines and a wild profusion of weeds
and grasses vied for space.

The outhouse's noisome stench assaulted my senses as I entered. Thick, entangled spider webs clung to the upper rafters and corners. A big-butted spider, black and menacing, guarded the opening where the boards did not quite join. I sat on one of the two round holes, shuddering at the maggots which worked ceaselessly in the liquefied mess below.

"Lawd, Sim, why don't you clean that thing out? Snake liable to bite your rump. Have mercy, Jesus."

Paris. Arrived yesterday. Saw Hemingway and Fitzgerald. Seemed to be in deep conversation. Wanted to ask them some questions. Decided not to. Later. Today, do the cafes. Walk on the Left Bank. My novel. Where is Stein? The Circle?

I walked back up the path, picked up the ax and headed down into the claypit and across the rock-hard red clay into the woods. Small to medium black jacks grew randomly on what was a hill situated up from Carpenter's Creek, where Grandma and Mama, at one time, washed our clothes and the clothes they took in to earn a few dimes toward household expenses.

I hacked at a medium-sized blackjack with uneven strokes, cut another one down, hefted them to my shoulders as I had seen Papa do, and staggered toward the house.

I dumped the two trees down at the chopping block and proceeded to chop them into the short sticks Mama needed for the stove, humming the "Habanera" from *Carmen*.

*I was standing on the stage of the
Metropolitan, bathed in the brilliant spot, my voice
lilting to goose-pimpling heights. "Love is a bird
that can't be tamed." My voice climbed the scale in a
dizzying display of vocal calisthenics. Silence.
Thundering applause. Cries of "Bravo!"
"Bravissimo!"*

"Child, where you been? Who tole you to
chop any wood? You go chop your foot off. Good
Gawd!"

I threw one shoulder back, lifted my chin,
grasped my skirt and shook it in the defiant
flounce of the flamenco dancer.

"Gal, is you crazy?"

 Ora Wills is an educator, editor, activist and historian.

She has edited and written for numerous volumes of the "When Black Folks Was Colored" series, an anthology of Southern life during the Jim Crow years. She is the editor of "Images in Black: A Pictorial History of Black Pensacola," and, in total, has edited seven books for the African American Heritage Society. She is also one of the founders of "Arts Quest," a nonprofit organization that exposes children to the performing and visual arts.

She still volunteers at area schools, even though much of her life has been spent in classrooms. She taught 46 years, and spent 23 of those years teaching English at Tate High School. She also taught at the University of West Florida for 12 years.

She is dedicated to improving the education of all children.

Made in the USA
Columbia, SC
30 November 2018